THERE IS NO TROUBLE
SO GREAT
THAT CANNOT BE
DIMINISHED BY
DOG KISSES

REAGANDOODLE & LITTLE BUDDY

SANDI SWIRIDOFF WITH WENDY DUNHAM

HARVEST HOUSE PUBLISHERS
EUGENE, OREGON

Cover design by Mary Eakin

Cover photo © Sandi Swiridoff

Interior design by Janelle Coury

Published in association with William K. Jensen Literary Agency, 119 Bampton Court, Eugene, Oregon 97404.

Reagandoodle and Little Buddy

Text copyright © 2018 by Sandi Swiridoff and Wendy Dunham
Photography copyright © by Sandi Swiridoff
Published by Harvest House Publishers
Eugene, Oregon 97408
www.harvesthousepublishers.com

ISBN 978-0-7369-7464-6 (Hardcover)
ISBN 978-0-7369-7465-3 (eBook)

Library of Congress Cataloging-in-Publication Data

Names: Swiridoff, Sandi, author. | Dunham, Wendy, author.
Title: Reagandoodle and little buddy / Sandi Swiridoff with Wendy Dunham.
Description: Eugene, Oregon : Harvest House Publishers, [2018]
Identifiers: LCCN 2017061384 (print) | LCCN 2018001557 (ebook) | ISBN 9780736974653 (ebook) | ISBN 9780736974646 (hardcover)
Subjects: LCSH: Labradoodle—Anecdotes. | Human-animal relationships. | Adoption—Anecdotes. | Foster home care—Anecdotes.
Classification: LCC SF429.L29 (ebook) | LCC SF429.L29 S95 2018 (print) | DDC 636.72/8—dc23
LC record available at https://lccn.loc.gov/2017061384

Printed in China

18 19 20 21 22 23 24 25 26 / RDS-JC / 10 9 8 7 6 5 4 3 2 1

Contents

. . . .

A Note from Sandi

. . . .

By profession, I'm a registered nurse. And because of my desire to help children in need, I started my career in pediatrics. But I'm also a wife, mother, Christian, friend, quick-witted punster, and passionate photographer who loves to bring joy to others through my photos. I have found symmetry and balance behind the camera lens. Photography is what energizes me and keeps me focused on the beautiful things in life. But in life, as in photography, focus can change. One day, without much notice, foster grandchildren entered my world, and I turned a corner to discover a wonderful new journey. Thus begins my @Reagandoodle story.

A few years have passed since then, but sometimes, when I think back on that period, I can still feel the bittersweet and raw tug of the emotions I experienced. My foster grandsons, whom I loved immeasurably, were getting ready to transition from my daughter's home to their adoptive home. My husband, Eric, and I had been their grandparents, Opa and DeeDee, for 18 months. We had been very involved in their lives, and now they were leaving us for their forever home. It was a beautiful but difficult time for our entire family. These two boys were my first foster grandchildren, and their adoption would leave a huge hole in my heart.

And so, as silly and cliché as it sounds, Eric and I thought a puppy might

help us fill the child-sized void we would soon experience. One Sunday afternoon we took a drive with our grandsons to "just look"' at a litter of Australian Labradoodle puppies. However, when we arrived, we discovered only one pup was left in the litter. As I reached down to pick up this little ball of fur, he licked my face. At that moment I knew he was going home with us. That was the day Reagan and I first met.

There is nothing quite like puppy therapy to get through a rough time. Reagan's spunk and playfulness helped us all. Our grandsons quickly latched on to the notion that we had "adopted" Reagan. We took that and ran with it, using Reagan's story as an example of real life adoption and how, even though he was sad to leave one family, he was welcomed with love and acceptance into his new family. The boys loved talking about Reagan's adoption as they prepared for their own.

There is nothing quite like puppy therapy to get through a rough time.

The weeks flew by, and before I knew it my foster grandsons had transitioned to their new home. Thankfully, Reagan was there to help ease my heartache. He gave me something to focus on (pun intended), loving my camera as much as my camera loved him. We were a match made in heaven. After posting countless photos of Reagan on Facebook, my family suggested an Instagram account for him. I was an Instagram rookie, knowing not a thing about this social networking app, but I was hooked after I viewed some amusing and quirky dog accounts. And so @Reagandoodle premiered in August 2014 when Reagan was six months old.

In the first four months, @Reagandoodle grew to more than 10,000 followers. I was fascinated with the creative design process and began to produce more imaginative photo/video shoots of my precocious pup. Reagan's IG followers climbed in numbers. When Reagan was 11 months old, a new foster grandson entered my life, Little Buddy. Coincidentally, he was also 11 months old, just like Reagan. From the moment they first met, Reagan and Little Buddy have been the best of friends. Reagan always brings a smile to Little Buddy's face and elicits endless giggles. Watching their bond warms my heart, as they have the same energy level and personality. I began to share glimpses of their special relationship through photos, never directly displaying Little Buddy's face and always respecting his privacy as a child in foster care. The images of Reagan and Little Buddy soon became my most popular posts on Instagram, and the number of followers continued to increase. Comments left on the posts indicated that the photos touched hearts and often made people laugh. Eventually, the photos caught the attention of several media outlets and were shared globally, along with our story.

Watching their bond warms my heart, as they have the same energy level and personality.

My Instagram account has raised public awareness and focused attention on the needs of children in foster care. The sale of my yearly Reagandoodle calendars gives me the opportunity and privilege to donate all proceeds to be used to enhance the lives of foster children and their families. It was Reagan's IG fan base that inspired me to seek publication for this book, with his and Little Buddy's story delightfully narrated by Reagandoodle himself. It serves as a great opportunity to give even more to my foster child campaign.

Reagan and Little Buddy have brought so much joy to my life, as have all of my foster grandchildren. I never imagined that a dog and an Instagram account would tie my passions together and impact hundreds of thousands of people along the way. I am thrilled to be able to share our story with you.

Sandi

A Word from My Daughter, Kari

. . . .

Foster care is hard but worth it. The kids are worth it. They are worthy of love, safety, care, and opportunity in the same way every child is. And while foster care is not necessarily something every family should dive head first into, I do believe every family can support foster families in some way. Bring them a meal, offer to babysit or have a playdate, be a listening ear, pray for them, and encourage foster parents as often as you think of them. You can just bring a pint of ice cream and sit together. The more support we can surround foster families with, the better.

They are worthy of love, safety, care, and opportunity in the same way every child is.

Because of fear, or the potential pain of a child leaving your family, I often hear, "I could never do it." And I get it! But I always go back to remind myself that, frankly, it's not about me. I hear, "It's not a good time for us," and then God reminds me, "It's not a good time for this child." There is pain and hardship in fostering, but there is also so much beauty and redemption. The need is great in every part of the country, so look into your local foster care system to see what you can do to help. My husband and I can say without hesitancy that fostering is one of the best things we've ever been a part of.

Kari

1

A Dog's Best Friend

If you live to be a hundred,
I want to live to be a hundred minus one day
so I never have to live a day without you.

WINNIE-THE-POOH

. . . .

I've heard it said that dogs are a man's best friend. That's because we're affectionate, good listeners, and extremely loyal to our humans. But if a canine's opinion accounts for anything, I say a dog's best friend is his boy. That's how it's been for me, anyway, at least since I was 11 months old. That's when I first saw Little Buddy. Once we met, I felt as though my whole world fell into place, as though I'd suddenly discovered my life's purpose—to look after him.

Because I was adopted as a pup, I felt I understood what Little Buddy was going through as a foster child. I've been around long enough (twenty-some dog years), to know there are certain things in life that no one can fully understand unless they've traveled that same path. And being adopted or fostered are two things which fall into that category. To make sure Little Buddy had the best possible transition into foster care, I promised myself I'd help him walk that path. I knew there would be times when I'd have to lead, and others when I'd trail behind. More often, I hoped we'd walk with each other side by side, the way friends do. I promised Little Buddy that wherever he needed me, I'd be there. And one thing was certain. I would never leave.

The first day I met Little Buddy, I knew we were a team. Although he was 11 months old too, I was bigger. And it just so happened that when I was on all fours, Little Buddy and I were the perfect height for giving kisses. And that was the very first thing I did when I saw him—I gave him a kiss (which coming from me, was more like a lick). After I'd kissed him, he wrapped his arms around my neck and kissed me back. Even though Little Buddy hadn't begun talking, I could tell he liked me too.

The first day I met Little Buddy, I knew we were a team.

Since I'd fallen instantly in love with him, I was also very much afraid. Because of all the things I'd already learned about children who are fostered, there was one thing in particular I knew well—they don't always stay forever. So my prayer the day Little Buddy and I met was that we would be together for a long time—even past the time he turned into a man. Perhaps when he'd be 35 or even 40, I thought. Because I hoped someday, many years from now, I would hear him say, "Reagan?" Then I'd look up at him as he scratched behind my ear. "I want you to know something." Then he would point to his chest and say, "You're this man's best friend!" And, of course, he'd know he was mine. We wouldn't need words for that.

Our story began long before that very first day when Little Buddy and I met...probably close to two years. So if you'll pull up a chair and lend me your ears, I'll share our true story about life and the love between a dog and his boy.

Well, at least it's mostly true. A dog can dream, right?

2

Life Changes

If nothing ever changed, there'd be no butterflies.

Author Unknown

. . . .

My full name is Reagandoodle, but almost everyone calls me Reagan. And if you know anything about dogs, you've probably guessed I'm a Labradoodle. And you would be right...or at least partially right. Technically, I'm an Australian Labradoodle. That means my breed has been refined by research and careful selection for more than 15 years. As you humans say, hard work pays off. And it did. It led to me, a well-bred, finespun, sophisticated Australian Labradoodle. We're known for our high levels of intuition, a goofy, fun-loving nature, and a need to belong as a family member.

I was born on February 23, 2014, in the town of Estacada, Oregon, which is about 30 miles southeast of Portland. Although Estacada is known for many things, I especially appreciate its history for growing Christmas trees because Christmas just happens to be dear to my heart.

Despite the fact I was born in a heated barn, the farm still grew chilly during the winter months. I remember keeping warm with my six siblings as we huddled together in a big puppy bundle, paws and tails entwined. Mother curled around us like a soft woolen blanket. We stayed with her for the first eight weeks of life. After that, things began to change.

At the end of those eight weeks, my siblings and I were old enough to leave. Mother explained that we'd soon be adopted and that we'd receive a new family—a family that would take us in and love us as their own. At first I didn't understand. I couldn't imagine why I'd need a new family when I already had one—one I loved and that loved me back. But even so, I tried not to worry. Mother taught us that worry has a way of giving small things a big shadow, and I certainly didn't want to create unnecessary shadows.

After those eight weeks, visitors came to see us—humans I'd never seen before. They came one at a time, in couples, and even as whole families. They chased us around the barn and threw balls, hoping we'd run after them. They even gave us belly rubs. We were picked up and carefully turned around, over, and upside down as they talked about our markings, the size of our ears, or the color of our fur. They discussed which of us was their favorite, and which one seemed the healthiest, the most energetic, or the most engaging. Sometimes they argued and had to come to an agreement over who they liked best. That's when I put two and two together—these people had come to adopt us. They wanted one of us to be part of their family.

They wanted one of us to be part of their family.

Over the next few days, I watched each of my siblings get chosen. When visitors came, they usually left with one of them. The humans were all nice, mind you. You could tell by the way they handled us—delicately and gingerly, as if we were bone china teacups. I had no doubt my siblings would be loved. Still, it was difficult to watch them go. I didn't know if I'd ever see them again.

I remember asking Mother why people were adopting her babies. She looked at me with her dark brown eyes and said, "Sometimes a mother cannot keep her children, but it doesn't mean she loves them any less." Then she

touched her nose against mine. "Son, life and love are often complicated. One day when you are a man dog, you will understand."

Still, I couldn't decide if I was the fortunate one who would get to stay with Mother forever, or, since I was the only pup left, that maybe I was the runt no one wanted. But because I felt normal otherwise—and from what I could see I looked like my siblings, and I had all four paws, thick handsome fur, and a tail that wagged nicely—I concluded I wasn't the runt but rather the fortunate one. The one who would stay with Mother forever.

I concluded I wasn't the runt but rather the fortunate one.

I Get Adopted

The last will be first, and the first last.

MATTHEW 20:16 HCSB

. . . .

One sunny April day when spring was busy waking the earth, a group of four humans came to see me. The two bigger ones were a husband and wife who referred to themselves as Eric and Sandi. They brought two young boys they said were their foster grandchildren. Right away I liked them all. Eric and Sandi, who the boys called Opa and DeeDee, were especially nice. They picked me up confidently, which made me feel safe. Sandi kept repeating how adorable I was (which I certainly didn't mind). She even compared my fur to the color of a caramel latte, saying it looked as if I had splashes of frothy milk on my paws, chest, neck, muzzle, and even the top of my head. Although I had no idea what a caramel latte was at the time, I remember how I liked being described as one.

I also really liked the boys. They were energetic and inquisitive, like me. They were also loud and fast moving, but since I'd spent my first eight weeks of life on a farm, I'd become accustomed to things like that. With a handful of cows, a few sheep, and a donkey, there was always some kind of commotion.

The boys took turns holding me, so back and forth between the two I went. They were as careful as children can be but still required the help of their Opa or

DeeDee to hold me, which was reassuring for a pup. As much as I loved being held and cuddled by them, a part of me feared I might accidently be dropped.

And then Sandi took me in her soft, warm hands. "Now it's my turn," she said. She lifted me up high, right in front of her face. I was so happy I wagged my tail as fast as I could and then kissed her—right on her nose. I remember how hard she laughed. That's when she looked at Eric and said, "He's perfect!" Upon hearing those words, I had an exciting yet slightly fearful thought...I was about to be adopted.

I was so happy I wagged my tail as fast as I could and then kissed her—right on her nose.

Sandi carefully set me down beside my mother. "Go ahead and say goodbye," she said. "Take as long as you need." So that's what I did. I nuzzled close to Mother, knowing I'd soon be gone. She leaned over and stroked my head with her soft, warm tongue, letting me know how much she loved me. After a few moments, she leaned in close and whispered, "Son, always remember—the last shall be first." I will never forget how special that made me feel. Being the last pup chosen, it was hard not feeling that there was something wrong with me. But Mother had a way of making me feel special.

I was then gently picked up by the same hands that had set me down to say goodbye and carried to the car that would take me to my new home in Portland, where I'd be part of a new family. Eric and Sandi would be my new dad and mom. I figured the boys would also be part of my family, but I wasn't sure just how.

As soon as Sandi and Eric placed me in the car, I heard Mother's owner, The Mrs., running toward us and yelling, "Don't leave without his blanket!" Then she placed it beside me where I was nestled between the boys. I immediately took a whiff. It held the comforting scents of my mother and siblings. Aside from my memories, my blanket was the only thing I had to remind me of home.

My New Home

*Nothing can bring a real sense of security
into the home except true love.*

BILLY GRAHAM

. . . .

Even though my new parents were incredibly kind throughout my adoption, the transition was still challenging. Everything I'd ever known was gone—my birth mother, my littermates, the farm. Everything was different. Now, everyone except me were humans. There were new faces, a whole new set of smells—none of which resembled life on a farm—and new food to adjust to (like almond milk lattes and gourmet peanut butter dog bones). There were even new rules—like no going to the bathroom on the carpet (I didn't even know what a carpet was until then), or no going to the bathroom anywhere in the house, for that matter.

That first day Eric and Sandi brought me home, they let me wander through the house and explore. As I did, the boys followed close behind, right on my tail. I went in every room, looked behind every door, and peeked in every closet. I sniffed everything. I found it comforting to know my surroundings. When we do, it isn't so likely we'll become lost or feel afraid.

After I'd explored the house and then played outside with the boys, it was time for them to take their nap. They obeyed my new mom well as she guided them into the spare bedroom, where they shared a bed. Curious, I followed. While Mom tucked them in—and while they were finally still—I took notice of their human fur. It was as shiny and black as something called patent leather. It seemed like a special kind of fur, different than I'd seen before. And it was different from Sandi's. Hers was a beautiful golden yellow, which reminded me of the evening sun that spread across our barnyard meadow. Thinking of home gave me a sensation of homesickness I wasn't accustomed to.

Thinking of home gave me a sensation of homesickness I wasn't accustomed to.

After kissing the boys on their foreheads, Sandi tucked me under her arm, carried me back out the door, and set me down.

Eric and Sandi had purchased a bed for me, which I thought was very generous. I imagined that not all pups were as fortunate. It was oblong and brownish, about the color of me. It looked so comfortable that I laid down and discovered that it was the softest bed I'd ever been on. And it was all mine. Sandi spread my blanket over me and tucked in the edges. Although I'd only planned on lying there for a minute, I realized how tired I was from the drive, from all the sniffing and exploring I'd done, and from playing with the boys. As I lay snuggled in my new bed with the scent of my mother and siblings wrapped around me, I fell asleep.

Little did I know that one day I would meet my very best friend in this home.

5

More New Family

You don't choose your family.
They are God's gift to you, as you are to them.

DESMOND TUTU

. . . .

The next thing I knew, I woke to the sound of people coming in the front door. Although they made a great deal of noise, it turned out there were only two of them. I didn't jump up or bark, but instead pretended to still be asleep. I carefully peeked out from beneath my blanket and watched as they hugged Mom and Dad, and then I watched some more as Mom and Dad hugged them back.

The two people were adults, probably in their early twenties by human years. Mom and Dad called the girl, Kari, and the boy, Zach. It turned out that Kari and Zach were married to each other. I then discovered that Kari and Zach were the foster parents of the two boys, who they had been fostering for the past 15 months.

It was when I heard Kari say, "It's good to see you, Mom and Dad!" that everything clicked. I realized that because Kari was my mom and dad's daughter, then she would be my new sister. And because she was married to Zach, that made him my brother-in-law (which I thought was very cool since I'd never had a brother-in-law). And the boys? Well, despite the fact they were older and bigger than me, I realized they were my foster nephews and I their foster uncle. Initially, it all seemed complicated. But it wasn't long until everything felt as comfortable as an old pair of jeans (which I can say with certainty, because it wasn't long before I began to wear them).

Still peeking from beneath my blanket, I watched Mom lead Kari and Zach toward my bed. "You won't believe what we did today," Mom said. "We adopted a puppy. Come see how adorable he is!" At that, I pulled my head under my blanket and held my breath—don't ask me why. Maybe it was because I felt shy and nervous knowing I was about to meet my new sister and brother-in-law.

A few seconds later, Mom lifted my blanket. The moment Kari set eyes on me, she reached down and scooped me up. "Oh my goodness!" she exclaimed. "He's the sweetest thing ever!" She tucked me beneath her chin and held me tight. I remember feeling such comfort. It felt good to have a sister again. After that hug, she turned to our mom and said, "I know he's precious, but why did you get a puppy? They're so much work. Besides, you've been down that road before. I remember you saying you'd never get another one."

I wasn't sure what a Reagandoodle was supposed to look like, but I was glad she liked my name. I liked it too.

Mom was quiet for a moment. Then she said, "I needed him. When you told me the boys would be moving to their forever family in three months, the sadness was hard for me to bear." She looked at Dad. "We figured a puppy would help fill the empty spot that will be left when they're gone."

Kari stroked my ears and nodded. "You're right. We're all going to need this little guy." Then she shifted me to the crook of her arm and cradled me like a baby. "What did you name him?"

"Reagandoodle."

Kari laughed. "Reagandoodle? I like it! He even looks like a Reagandoodle." I wasn't sure what a

Reagandoodle was supposed to look like, but I was glad she liked my name. I liked it too.

While Kari held me, the door to the spare bedroom flew open. Within seconds the boys were at her side, jumping up to touch me. "Mama Kari, Mama Kari!" the older boy shouted. "Opa and DeeDee got a puppy! They adopted him—just like me and my brother will be adopted!" Kari and Mom instantly exchanged a look. It was a look I understood. Although I was only eight weeks old, I already had a keen understanding of life. By observing the boys since I'd arrived, I'd grown aware that kids often know more than adults realize.

And just look at how he's already loved.

Kari bent down to meet him at eye level. "You're right," she said. Then she brushed his patented leather hair away from his face. "And just look at how he's already loved."

That five-year-old little boy smiled and patted me on the head. "I know. He sure is loved a lot!" His younger brother, who was two-years-old, liked imitating his big brother and piped in, "He loved a lot!"

After staying a while longer to play with me, Kari said it was time for her and Zach to take the boys home. I didn't want them to go, but Kari assured me that they lived close and promised they would be back the next weekend.

I wasn't sure I could wait.

6

Empty Spots

Show me your hands. Do they have scars from giving?
Show me your feet. Are they wounded in service?
Show me your heart. Have you left a place for divine love?

FULTON J. SHEEN

· · · · · · · · · · · ·

The following week, after I'd begun getting used to my new parents and surroundings, Kari and Zach came back with the boys just as she promised. They arrived right after lunch, so the boys and I had time to play before their nap. Since I sensed Kari needed a little peace and quiet, I was glad we could play outside. Even though she was smiling and looked as though everything was fine, I saw tension in her neck. Not everyone notices things like that. But as I mentioned, Australian Labradoodles are highly intuitive. So to provide her with quietness, I went to the door and pawed at the bell Mom had hung for me. That was how I let her know I wanted to go out.

I remember running around the yard with the boys until we were tuckered out. We played fetch, tag, and even Doggie, Doggie, Where's Your Bone? all before Mom and Kari called us in for a snack. The boys had graham crackers and apple juice, while I had peanut butter dog bones. I also enjoyed the small bits of the boys' crackers that accidently fell to the floor. I'd decided that picking up all dropped pieces of food would be my responsibility. Puppies (as well as children) are never too young to contribute to the greater good of their household. Everyone can do something, be it big or small. I would manage the crumbs.

After washing the sticky juice off the boys, Mom said she'd tuck them in for their nap. But first she put water on to boil and asked that Kari make them tea, which I felt would be good for Kari. From observing my people, I'd learned that drinking tea with someone you love somehow had a way of making the world feel whole again. Not that I thought Kari's world had suddenly crumbled upon her, but I'd learned that sometimes life, mixed with its unpredictable beats, can make it seem as though it has.

I'd learned that drinking tea with someone you love somehow had a way of making the world feel whole again.

The house was quiet. The boys were sleeping, Dad and Zach were in the garage working on a project, and Kari and Mom were at the table, the scents of mint and chamomile tea wafting around us. I was under the table, lying in my favorite afternoon sun patch with my eyes closed, enjoying the warmth. Although I was not intentionally eavesdropping, I was privy to the conversation between Mom and Kari.

Well, Kari did all the talking, so maybe it really wasn't a conversation but rather more of a catharsis. It's been a while now, but here's what I remember hearing Kari say.

"Even though it's an honor to love and raise children from difficult places, it's one of the hardest things I've ever done. It's not just physically draining, but emotionally as well, and it's definitely taken a toll on Zach and me. On our patience, our faith, our marriage...every part of our lives." She paused and then went on. "But the children are worth it. They are worthy of a love that won't give up on them, worthy of a love that shows them what a healthy, albeit

imperfect, family looks like, and worthy of a love that will carry them through the tantrums, the heartache, and the confusion they deal with on a daily basis." Since Kari stopped to blow her nose, I suspected she was crying. "They are worth any pain I might go through, because it's not about me. And, honestly, fostering children has completed my heart more than I ever imagined it would."

After hearing that, I realized just how beautiful my sister was. I already knew she was beautiful to look at, but I began to be aware of the beauty she had in places I couldn't see. And this made me love her even more.

"Well," Mom said, "I think your weekend get-away will do both you and Zach a world of good. And don't worry about the boys. They have Reagan to play with."

Kari slid her chair back and stood up. "Speaking of the boys, I'd better wake them and say goodbye. Zach and I want to reach the cabin before sunset."

"Good idea," said Mom. "The boys will have so much fun, they won't know you're gone."

And that's exactly what we did with the boys that weekend (and over the next three months they were still with Kari and Zach)—we had fun. They stayed for sleepovers, we played our favorite board games, and we snuggled together under blankets as we watched movies and shared popcorn. We even scrunched together for "rub-a-dub-dub, three-men-in-a-tub" baths. Even though these baths resulted in a big, splashy mess, Mom never seemed to mind.

Over those three months, we showed the boys how wonderful adoption can be. Because of my adoption, they witnessed how loved I was, and they saw that my needs were always met. They also realized how much Mom and Dad wanted me, which, personally, I think is one of the most incredible things I've learned about adoption. Because it's a

Because it's a choice, anyone who is adopted can be certain they're wanted...and that is a very good feeling.

choice, anyone who is adopted can be certain they're wanted...and that is a very good feeling.

Before we knew it, those three months were gone, and it was time for the boys to move to their forever family. It was time to say goodbye. The boys taught me something I will never forget: It's okay to love someone even though it may not be forever. I'm still grateful we allowed ourselves to love each other.

After they left, my family seemed happy and sad at the same time. I know I was. It can be complicated when two feelings are mixed together. We knew the boys would be loved, cared for, and wanted by their new family, but the rest of us were left with empty spots—and they were big. I've learned that empty spots can be difficult to fill. They are like wide, deep wounds that require time, ointment, and a regular change of bandages. And although they eventually close up and fill in, their marks remain, subtle and pink, a reminder of love and a life once shared.

That's what foster care does. It changes lives.

We had changed the lives of two little boys, and they had changed ours.

That's what foster care does. It changes lives.

7

More Than Just a Photo Shoot

A kind heart is a fountain of gladness,
making everything in its vicinity freshen into smiles.

WASHINGTON IRVING

. . . .

It was around that same time, in August 2014, when I'd finally worn that comfortable pair of jeans I mentioned. That's because it was then when Mom began dressing me up and taking pictures of me. She dressed me in human clothes, which I thought was great fun.

Taking pictures together was something special Mom and I shared. It was a bonding experience for us, kind of a "Mom and Me" time, which I valued. Her setting apart time just for me made me feel extra special. Plus, as an added benefit, I received treats. Mom knew I loved freeze-dried liver treats, so that's what she gave me. Because I enjoyed them, I didn't let on that I really didn't need them. I was already used to the camera. Mom had been taking pictures of me from the moment I was adopted.

Because I looked so adorable in the pictures, Mom posted them to her Facebook account. After more and more people liked my pictures, Kari and our brother, Justin (who you haven't been introduced to yet), encouraged

Mom to create an Instagram account just for me, which she did. I'd never dreamed of having my own Instagram account. And I'd never dreamed I would be so popular either. But looking back, what I remember valuing the most was that my pictures—pictures of me (a regular canine from Oregon)—made people smile.

Even though it was Kari and Justin who encouraged Mom to create an account for me in the first place, they initially seemed a bit embarrassed and even teased Mom for going overboard as they watched her become a "crazy dog lady" who paired dog photos with captions using silly puns. I remember watching them roll their eyes. But all in all, when Kari and Justin saw my popularity skyrocket, I sensed no hesitation in their support of our fun-loving and creative mom. It seemed everyone in our family saw how much she enjoyed using her talents to bring joy to others. I know I did.

It seemed everyone in our family saw how much she enjoyed using her talents to bring joy to others. I know I did.

Whenever Mom received a compliment on her photos of me, I'd hear her explain time and time again how she loved using her talent to brighten other people's lives and to bring them hope. Knowing I had a part in that made me feel good about myself. So even if I never received another treat for dressing up and doing my best to smile at the camera, I remember knowing in my heart that I would do it anyway.

8

Puffy Orange Pumpkin

I can smell autumn dancing in the breeze.
The sweet chill of pumpkin and crisp sunburnt leaves.

AUTHOR UNKNOWN

. . . .

The tail end of that summer passed, and we were well into the swing of autumn when Mom began talking about a holiday called Halloween. Because I was only eight months old at the time, I'd never experienced Halloween. Apparently, human children (which according to Mom included me), dressed up in costumes and went door-to-door with decorated bags or plastic pumpkins, asking for candy.

I recall not liking the sounds of that for two reasons. First of all, asking (truthfully, more like begging) went against everything I'd been taught. Ever since I'd been a pup, if I were to whine while my humans were eating food that looked delicious, I'd usually hear the words, "Don't beg!" So I did not like begging. Second, since I'd been taught that dogs are not allowed to eat candy, I had no desire to go door-to-door begging for something I couldn't eat. Instead, Mom agreed we could stay home, where I would help her answer the door and hand out candy. As far as the dressing up part was concerned, I was already used to that.

Mom had chosen my costume weeks in advance but wouldn't tell me what it was. I think she wanted to surprise me. I tried to imagine what she would dress me as...maybe a cowboy or a farmer. Or possibly even a lion. But on the evening of October 31, Mom dressed me in my surprise costume, and I was embarrassingly dressed as a pumpkin—a puffy orange pumpkin with a beanie pumpkin-stem hat. Thankfully, seconds after I'd been transformed into that pumpkin, the doorbell began ringing, and I forgot how silly I felt. When I went to the door, I counted five children on our door step. They were dressed in all kinds of costumes—fairies, witches, and clowns, and who loudly shouted, "Trick-or-treat!"

I did not like that, so I barked at them.

"Halloween's almost over, Reagan, so for what my brotherly advice is worth, you might as well let Mom have her fun."

I heard Mom tell Dad she thought I was afraid of the costumes, but that was not the case. I had only barked because I was trying to tell the children it was not polite to beg. That was when Mom and Dad decided to take over. I was made to sit on the couch, still dressed as a pumpkin, and watch.

Kari and Zach stopped over to say hello and ended up helping Mom and Dad pass out the last of the candy. Justin also stopped by with his wife, Danielle. They were on their way to a Halloween party, so they didn't stay long. I remember sitting on the couch, feeling like a pumpkin set out on the front steps, when Kari told me how cute I looked. Danielle agreed. Zach, on the other hand, looked at me with sympathy and sighed. "It's okay, Reagan-D." He often called me that. "You'll look like your old self in no time!" A brother-in-law was a valuable family member to have. Then Justin sided with Zach. "Halloween's almost over, Reagan, so for what my brotherly advice is worth, you might as well let Mom have her fun."

I took his advice. And after thinking about it, I'd decided that being dressed as a pumpkin wasn't really so bad. I knew Mom would post my Halloween pictures on Instagram, and they would brighten someone's day. Over the years, I've learned that a little bit of sacrifice often brings great dividends.

Although no one spoke it out loud, I imagined everyone was thinking the same thing I was—what fun it would have been to take the two boys trick-or-treating. I wondered if they had gone trick-or-treating with their new family, and I tried to imagine what they might have dressed up as.

We were beginning to heal.

Although we still needed bandages to cover our empty spots, we didn't need as much ointment as we did before. We were beginning to heal.

9

A Healthy Balance

Life is like a bicycle.
To keep your balance, you must keep moving.

ALBERT EINSTEIN

. . . .

Thanksgiving came and went, and Christmas arrived. The snow caused me to feel nostalgic as I thought about Estacada and the farm. I wondered how my birth mother was. I wondered where my siblings were, what their families were like, and if they were as happy as I was.

One Sunday afternoon in the middle of December, I remember Mom and Dad saying it was time to get our Christmas tree. They made sure to bundle me up because we were to hike out to a field and cut our own tree. When we got in the car, Dad announced we were going to Estacada to get our tree—back to the town where I was born. On our way, I wondered what it would be like to stop by the farm and possibly see my birth mother.

Shortly after passing the "Welcome to Estacada" sign, things began to look familiar. Our car slowed down, and Dad pulled into the driveway of a big farmhouse. When I first saw it, the house's shape looked familiar, and I began to get excited, thinking that maybe Dad had also thought about stopping at the farm. But when I saw the house was gray, and not white as I remembered, I felt a twinge of disappointment, thinking that maybe it wasn't the farmhouse after all. But as Dad pulled up to the side door and The Mrs., my birth mother's owner, stepped out, I realized it was the right farmhouse—someone had simply painted it. While The Mrs. walked toward our car, I wagged my tail and barked as loud as I could. It felt so good to see her.

As The Mrs. bent down and looked in Dad's window, her face lit up. "My goodness, what a welcome surprise! How nice to see you folks!" Dad rolled down the window. As she bent down further to look behind him, our eyes met. I could tell she remembered me. She reached in, rubbed my ear, and then smiled as she shook her head. "My, how he's grown. And his name?"

Mom leaned across Dad. "Reagandoodle," she answered. "But for the most part—unless he gets himself in mischief—he's simply Reagan."

> "What a handsome fella he turned out to be."

The Mrs. nodded with approval. "Reagandoodle," she said, almost to herself. "What a handsome fella he turned out to be." I barked, wishing I could thank her for the compliment. Then she rubbed her chin as if she were trying to recall something. "And if I remember correctly, he was the last of the litter to go."

I barked again, only louder. How I wanted to tell her what my birth mother had said—that the last shall be first.

Dad asked if we could go inside the barn to see my birth mother.

The Mrs. shook her head sympathetically. "I'm sorry, but she's on an errand with The Mr., and I don't expect they'll be back for some time. He had to get a load of straw from the Walkers' farm, and she likes to ride along." Then she chuckled. "The Walkers have a handsome Irish setter, and I believe she has her eyes on him."

Mom and Dad laughed too. I tried but couldn't. First, because dogs can't laugh, and second, I was feeling sad since I couldn't see my birth mother. While the adults kept at their small talk, I quietly sat back onto my seat. I remember

taking several deep breaths to help ease my disappointment. But after thinking about it a little more, I decided I'd be okay. At least I got to see The Mrs. And even though I couldn't see my birth mother right then, she was in my heart and I knew I was in hers. I reminded myself to do my best to focus on the present, and that is exactly what I did. I kept my chin up and remembered what we'd set out to do in the first place—to get our Christmas tree. I couldn't wait to bring it home and help decorate.

Looking back, I feel I gained a lot from that experience. I learned that, for the most part, life is best lived while facing forward—kind of like riding a bicycle. When pedaling forward, we move ahead in our journey with relative ease. But when we try to maneuver backward, it's difficult to steer, and our perception can become skewed. It was the day when we visited the farm that I decided I'd try my best to live life while facing forward. I understood there would be times I would need to look back, because our past is just as important as our future. But for the most part, I would try to live in the present. I decided for me, that choice made for a healthy balance.

> *I learned that, for the most part, life is best lived while facing forward— kind of like riding a bicycle.*

10

My First Christmas

He who has not Christmas in his heart
will never find it under a tree.

Roy L. Smith

. . . .

Christmas Eve with Mom and Dad was special. It was our first Christmas together as a family. In addition, it was the first Christmas I'd experienced. Mom put on Christmas music while she and Dad strung popcorn and cranberries. I remember wanting to string popcorn and cranberries with them, but my paws simply weren't designed for such fine work. Instead, I decided I'd help by eating every piece of popcorn Mom and Dad dropped. Once they finished stringing the popcorn and berries, they wove the strands through the branches (but only those near the top). Back then, when I was full of even more mischief than now, they had to make a lot more accommodations for me. Next, they hung the ornaments. I remember how beautiful our tree looked. But even more so, with all its popcorn and cranberries, it smelled delicious.

Kari and Zach and Justin and Danielle spent Christmas Day with us, which made Mom, Dad, and me very happy. There's something about the holidays that makes families want to be together. I remember thinking that Mom had made a big fuss over Halloween, but when Christmas arrived, she made an even bigger fuss. She decorated the house with pine boughs, holly berries, mistletoe, strings of twinkling lights, and a nativity set that she placed on the mantel, which Mom explained was the reason we celebrated Christmas.

One night of Advent, she took baby Jesus down from the mantel and explained that he was the King of the world. At the time, I remember thinking he looked too small to be a king. But just like puppies, I imagined babies grew up too. And later I discovered that's exactly what happened.

One of the most incredible things about that Christmas was the meal Mom prepared. I'll never forget those wonderful smells. She made stuffed Cornish game hens with a cranberry and thyme sauce, wild rice pilaf, ginger cashew green beans, candied sweet potatoes, and homemade rolls. How I wished I could sit at the table with the rest of the family. But at least Mom gave me a sampling in my food dish—a few pieces of meat, along with a handful of green beans and several bites of sweet potatoes. Simply thinking about that meal still makes me drool.

After dinner, everyone collapsed on the couch complaining how full they were and how they shouldn't have eaten so much. Were I able to talk, I'd have politely informed them about portion control. But as full as they were, everyone managed to move around enough to exchange gifts. Each member of the family gave special gifts and received some too. Even me. I was given a stocking filled with chew toys, dog treats shaped like candy canes, a set of red and green tennis balls, and a five-pound box of gourmet dog bones. As I pulled the items out of my stocking, I thought about the boys and wished they were with us too. I imagined the three of us playing fetch with my new tennis balls. Yet at the same time I felt confident they were with their own family, happy and celebrating Christmas like me. Although I missed them terribly and thought of them often, I no longer had to wear a bandage on my empty spot. No one else did either.

Don't get me wrong, our empty spots were still there. But they were healing, just like they were meant to.

11

Little Buddy and Me: Friends at First Sight

As soon as I saw you, I knew an adventure was going to happen.

WINNIE-THE-POOH

. . . .

One snowy day when we were halfway through January, I'd noticed that Mom and Dad seemed unusually excited. They'd woken up earlier than normal. Dad shoveled the driveway while Mom rushed about the house, cleaning. She'd also made a special breakfast. Pancakes for Dad and herself, and for me she'd made my favorite—woofles. As I swallowed my last bite, Mom explained that Kari and Zach would be coming over, and they were bringing someone special for me to meet—a new child they'd begun to foster. And that someone special just happened to be an 11-month-old boy named Little Buddy.

I remember being so excited that I ran to the entryway front door and sat down. I waited and waited and would not move until Little Buddy came through the door. I was more than ready to make sure he felt safe, wanted, and, most of all, loved.

Although it was only a matter of minutes, it seemed I'd been waiting at the door for hours. Finally, Kari and Zach's vehicle pulled into our driveway. I watched through the glass as Zach lifted a small boy from the backseat who was (except for his face) completely wrapped and bundled in winter gear.

I remember barely being able to contain myself as they came through our door.

This is, by far, one of my fondest memories.

I was always happy when Kari and Zach came over, but that day was exceptionally exciting. And I could tell Little Buddy was just as excited—he was quite wiggly and seemed to have a difficult time holding still long enough to be unbundled. But the moment he was free from his jacket, leggings, hat, scarf, boots, and mittens, Little Buddy and I stood face-to-face. Of course, Zach was holding him upright. Little Buddy was only 11 months old and still wobbly on his feet. We looked at each other for a moment, and then Little Buddy smiled the biggest smile I think I'd ever seen. That was when I gave him a kiss, and when he wrapped his arms around me and kissed me right back. This is, by far, one of my fondest memories.

After Little Buddy and I said hello, Zach eased him to the floor and he began to crawl—all around the house. I remember how curious he was. Just like me when I first came there. Little Buddy wanted to know what was beyond our entryway. He wanted to see everything. And I decided to show him.

Although it wasn't technically his house, I figured Little Buddy would be spending a lot of time with us. He wouldn't need his own bedroom, like he had at Zach and Kari's, but I figured he'd have plenty of naps and sleepovers in our spare bedroom, so I decided to show him that first. I let him look under the bed, inside the closet, and even behind the door. I let him take as long as he needed. I didn't want him to feel rushed. I remember feeling it was important for Little Buddy to know there weren't any monsters in our house (of course, I didn't believe in them). I recalled my first night of being adopted and how I'd been afraid. Thinking back, there really wasn't anything to be afraid of; things were just different. And sometimes when you're little, like Little Buddy was,

different is enough to be scary. When it was my first day, I remember how I'd gone from room to room, sniffing inside the closets, underneath the beds, and behind the doors just to check things out. I wanted Little Buddy to check things out too, so he would feel safe.

After I'd shown him the spare bedroom, we passed the hallway closet where Mom has always kept my basket of stuffed animals. That's when I got an idea. I thought it would be nice to give one of my toys to Little Buddy. I thought he might like to have one to hold and snuggle with. I knew it would be a comfort to him.

As I pushed the hallway closet door open with my paw, Little Buddy peeked in. I remember his eyes opening wide. I gently nudged him away from the door so I could get in; I didn't want to step on his fingers. Also, I remember how I wanted to choose the perfect stuffed animal. I could have given him my favorite—which was my teddy—but I was old enough to know that just because that was my favorite toy, it didn't mean it would be Little Buddy's. So I picked through the pile until I found the perfect one—my green-and-blue-striped snake. It was like new. I carefully lifted it by the edge and placed it by Little Buddy. But when I did, he picked it up and gave it back. I needed to make him understand I was giving it to him. I tried again. When I dropped it near him the second time, Mom looked at Kari and said, "I think Reagan is trying to give Little Buddy his snake!" I remember how good it felt to be understood.

After I'd given Little Buddy the snake, I showed him the rest of the main level. I led him to the living room, where Mom, Dad, and I watch TV. Right away, Little Buddy climbed up on the couch—which is exactly what I'd wanted him to do. I'd learned the importance in discovering how comfortable someone's couch is before making a commitment to sit and stay awhile. And since Little Buddy seemed to think our couch was comfortable, I figured he'd be happy to stay for a long time. I remember feeling excited. I knew it wouldn't be long before Little Buddy and I would be watching our favorite shows together.

He Has My Back Too

*Some people arrive and make
such a beautiful impact on your life
you can barely remember what
life was like without them.*

ANNA TAYLOR

. . . .

I also knew I would soon be acclimating Little Buddy to how we managed meals and snacks in our house. After he decided he liked our couch, I guided him to the dining room, where Mom and Dad ate their meals. As for me, I stayed under the table to mind my manners. After showing Little Buddy the dining room, I took him to the kitchen, which I'd come to know was an important room in our house. First, it was where Mom kept my stash of treats. Second, it was where she kept our latte maker.

I didn't want to overwhelm Little Buddy, so I decided to show him only the main level. Instead of going upstairs, I thought he might like a treat and drink of water. I'd learned from watching Mom that when someone comes to your home, it's polite to offer them something to eat and drink. Doing that, I decided, would be one more way I could help Little Buddy feel welcome.

I nudged his arm with my nose, hoping he'd follow. And he did, straight to the kitchen. Even though I was more than willing to share my treats with him, I'd learned from the two boys that humans prefer their own treats.

I wanted to get Little Buddy's snack all by myself, but since my paws weren't as dexterous as I preferred, I needed Mom's assistance. In order to get her help, I needed to get her attention. To do that, I decided to sit in front of the refridgerator and hope she noticed. Little Buddy followed suit and sat beside me.

Mom and Kari were on the other side of the kitchen talking, and neither of them seemed to notice me. Thankfully, Little Buddy stayed right beside me.

I wanted Little Buddy to have a snack, and I was not going to give up.

Still trying to get their attention, I swiped the fridge several times, hoping they'd hear. They did not. Little Buddy continued to wait patiently, as though he realized I was trying my best. Because I didn't want to make him wait any longer, I remember letting out one of my best barks—not the kind that signaled a true emergency, like "There's a squirrel in our backyard!" but one which meant I was serious. I wanted Little Buddy to have a snack, and I was not going to give up.

The very moment I barked, Mom and Kari rushed over. Mom looked surprised. "What's the matter, Reagan?" she asked. I swiped the fridge again. "You're hungry? Do you want a treat?" I barked once more and then nudged Little Buddy's shoulder. Mom turned to Kari. "Would you look at that. I think he wants Little Buddy to have a treat!"

Kari smiled. "I think so too. Reagan is nothing short of amazing."

I tried not to blush.

It was right then that the cutest thing happened—Little Buddy looked at Mom (or DeeDee as he learned to call her) and said, "Tweet." Of course, he meant *treat*, but I'd overheard Mom say that children Little Buddy's age aren't developmentally ready to pronounce the letter *r*. And the way Little Buddy

pronounced his, I thought, was one of the many things that made him so incredibly cute.

Mom and Kari prepared our snacks and set Little Buddy in his high chair. He was given the choice between crackers or apple slices. He chose apples. Having observed Mom and Kari with the two boys, I'd learned how important it is to give people choices—especially children. By giving choices, it allows children to feel that they've been heard. Even children as young as Little Buddy need to be heard. And if you'd like my opinion, that holds true for canines as well.

By giving choices, it allows children to feel that they've been heard.

For my snack, I chose my usual—all-natural peanut butter dog bones with a side of fresh water. While Little Buddy and I ate, he tried giving me an apple slice. Unfortunately, Mom saw. She explained to Little Buddy that the apples were for him and that I had my own snack. But as soon as Mom turned away, Little Buddy snuck me one. That's when I knew Little Buddy had my back too. That one small act by Little Buddy made me recall one of Mom's favorite Bible verses, Proverbs 27:9: "A sweet friendship refreshes the soul." And after having met Little Buddy, my soul was already feeling refreshed.

13

I Become a Mentor

I follow three rules: Do the right thing,
do the best you can, and always show people you care.

LOU HOLTZ

. . . .

In addition to showing Little Buddy around our house and offering him a snack, I decided it would be a good idea to let him in on some of the house rules I'd learned over the previous months. I remember thinking back to the very first rule I'd learned—no going to the bathroom on the carpet (or anywhere in the house for that matter). I then thought of how that rule might apply to Little Buddy. I remembered, however, that he was still at the age when human boys wear diapers. I also recalled that when it comes time for a human boy to transition from diapers, they learn to do their business while placed on a fancy seat (sometimes referred to as a throne, as Zach says). This fancy seat is big enough to hold several gallons of water. It also has an elegant handle that when pushed, sets the water (along with any business) into a swirling motion and then, somehow, quickly disappears. Fortunately, Little Buddy wouldn't need to concern himself with the first rule. Some rules, I'd learned, were only meant for dogs.

The second rule I remembered learning was that no muddy paws were allowed in the house. As a subtle reminder (I assumed for me), we had a mat outside our door that read "Wipe Your Paws!" Now, because he didn't have paws, that rule also wasn't technically a concern for him. I simply needed him to learn that when we came in from playing outside, he should remove his shoes or boots when they were wet or muddy or simply stomp his feet if they were dry. I, on the other hand, was always to wipe my paws. I'd come to learn that rules are important for everyone, whether adults, children, or canines. Rules provide us with order and have a way of making life more predictable. They help us feel secure, which I understood was especially important for children, and sometimes even more so for children going through change.

Having fun is important when you want to make someone feel at home.

I also decided that having Little Buddy learn only those two rules was the perfect place to start. I didn't want him to feel overwhelmed. Through observing Mom and Dad, as well as Kari and Zach, I'd learned that no child (or canine for that matter) should be expected to learn everything all at once— especially not a foster child. Kari had explained that they already have enough things they're trying to sort through. They're dealing with emotions, feelings, and worries others may not even be aware of. And all of that, she said, required a lot of energy. I, therefore, felt that having Little Buddy take several small steps would be more effective than having him take one or two giant leaps. Besides, I'd learned that little steps add up, so that eventually they equal big ones.

Next, I wanted to make sure Little Buddy had fun while he was at our house. Having fun is important when you want to make someone feel at home. (I'd learned that from watching Dad interact with the two boys when they were here. He always made sure they had fun.) I considered going outside in the snow with Little Buddy so we could play, but then I remembered children must be bundled up to go out in the cold. And when they are bundled, they cannot move. Since I figured Little Buddy wouldn't have much fun watching me

run circles around him, I tried showing Mom that we wanted to play inside. I chased Little Buddy around the dining table, under the chairs, and around the couch, but unfortunately, neither Mom nor Kari were keen on that idea. Looking back on the situation from their perspective, I now understand. With 40 clumsy pounds of canine fluff running around the house, someone could accidentally get hurt.

Instead, I decided to read books with Little Buddy, which was a much calmer activity. Because of Mom, I understood the value in reading and knew that reading together would help build Little Buddy's and my relationship. As it was, Little Buddy seemed to have a love for books. I think he'd have sat for hours as long as we had one between us. But since my paws were big and clumsy even back then, it was difficult for me to turn the pages. I gave that job to Little Buddy. I'm quite certain it made him feel special.

14

The Unknowns

If we keep our face to the sunshine, we cannot see the shadow.

HELEN KELLER

. . . .

The month of February, as I remember, was special. It was the month when Little Buddy and I both turned one. It was also the month for celebrating Valentine's Day.

Because Kari and Zach had just begun to foster Little Buddy, the two of us didn't have the opportunity to celebrate our first birthday together the way we've done ever since. Instead, I ended up celebrating with my teddy bear friends, and I had a special doggie cupcake Mom bought for me (which I embarrassingly ate in two seconds). Thankfully, Little Buddy ended up coming over on his birthday, and we celebrated with a bouquet of red heart balloons (which I helped Mom pick out). We wanted to show Little Buddy how much we loved him. Even though he was still very young at the time, I felt certain he knew.

That Valentine's Day I remember feeling especially thankful to have Little Buddy for my valentine. And I wanted him to be mine forever. But in my heart, I knew that wasn't realistic. Through watching Kari and Zach with the two boys, I had already learned about the unknowns.

The unknowns, I realized, were the hard realities of fostering. And one of the unknowns at the time was that no one knew how long Little Buddy would be with Kari and Zach. I'm sure dealing with the unknowns can be one of the most difficult things for a foster child, as I imagine it is for the birth parents. The unknowns can also be difficult for foster parents and their families. And they are difficult for dogs. The unknowns can make most anyone worry and feel anxious. There were times I felt that the ground beneath my paws was going to give way. I did not like the unknowns. I worried that Little Buddy would have to leave, that he would be returned to his biological family, or that he would be adopted by another family, as the two boys had been. To deal with the unknowns, I tried to manage them by living one day at a time...sometimes, by one moment at a time, and at others, by one breath at a time. I'd come to learn that, really, that is all any of us can count on. One day. One moment. One breath.

I'd come to learn that, really, that is all any of us can count on. One day. One moment. One breath.

Sometimes, when I began to worry if Little Buddy would have to leave us, I'd think about a magnet Mom kept on our refrigerator. It was big and square with fancy lettering. Mom often read it out loud, probably to remind herself too: "God, help me to remember that you are with us no matter what we face, that we can trust you when we cannot see, and that your plans are always greater than ours." Mom still has that magnet on our fridge, and those words still bring me peace.

Something else I'd learned about the foster care system is that not every child in the system is up for adoption. Sometimes, the goal for foster children is to be returned to their immediate family whenever possible, or at least to someone in their extended family. Each child's plan is different. And what I'd especially learned from Kari and Mom is that no matter what the child's plan may be, the job of the foster parents and their foster family is to support that child as their plan unfolds, whether it is to return to their biological family or

adoption. If adoption is decided, the whole process may take a long time—often longer than one thinks they can bear. A family may have a foster child with them for more than a year, and during that time bonds can become so strong it seems they will never be broken. But then, even after that length of time, even when there are plans for adoption, things may change.

Even though I'd learned and understood all of that, somehow my excitement of having Little Buddy with our family took over so that I forgot. I forgot that some things are not forever. I had much to learn. I had to prepare my heart to be happy for Little Buddy whatever his plan became. And just as I'd promised myself from the moment I met him, I knew I'd be there for him. No matter what.

As I'd promised myself from the moment I met him, I knew I'd be there for him. No matter what.

The boys had stayed with Kari and Zach for one and a half years. And then, after all that time, they had to leave. I realized I was supposed to be happy for them. They were going to have a forever family. And truthfully, I was happy for them. I was just sad for myself because I knew I'd miss them. I will never forget how painful it was when they left. As proof, I still have a pink area left from my empty spot. But because of this, I've learned that sometimes good things come about because of something sad—and I like to believe that is what happened with the boys. It was because the boys were to leave for their forever family that I was adopted. And despite our initial pain of saying goodbye to one another, it actually became a good situation for me as well as for the boys. I learned that like many things in life, it's our perspective that adjusts our light meter. So just like Mom does with her camera during our photo shoots, I always try keeping my light meter adjusted to the brightest setting.

Even so, I did not want to think about the unknowns. I wasn't sure I could live a single day without Little Buddy. Instead, I did my best to focus on the present—one day, one moment, one breath.

15

The Floater and a Field of Tulips

Look at me! Look at me!
Look at me NOW!
It is fun to have fun
But you have to know how.

DR. SEUSS

. . . .

There are two special places that hold extra fun memories for Little Buddy and me. The first is our annual Tulip Festival held at the Wooden Shoe Tulip Farm in Woodburn, Oregon, and the other is our second home, located on the Columbia River (please note I did not say *near* the river, but *on* it), which is why it is referred to as "the Floater."

Every April we attend the Tulip Festival. It is no doubt one of the most amazing events I've been to. In fact, the Tulip Festival was the first outing Mom and Dad took me on; we went the day following my adoption. The tulip farm was very different from the farm I was born on because the Tulip Farm raised tulips, not animals. What is most amazing, however, is that there are more than 40 acres of tulips to explore, and they are all planted neatly, in evenly spaced rows. And to a dog, this particular layout cries only one thing—RUN! What a thrill it is to run wild through a field of tulips. It is, in a word, exhilarating. My second trip to the Tulip Farm was shared with Little Buddy. Although I didn't run quite as fast when I was with him, I discovered there is nothing quite as fun as tiptoeing through a field of tulips with your bestie. To this day, the tulip remains my favorite flower.

Looking back when I was first adopted, I'd heard Mom and Dad talk about the house on the river. But since I hadn't been there yet, I had little concept of what a river house was. In my mind, I pictured a tiny house fastened to the top of a huge pile of inflatable water toys, like alligators, sea turtles, and dolphins.

Imagine a place surrounded by tranquil water the color of a border collie's eyes...

It wasn't long before I discovered I wasn't too far off. The Floater is, in fact, a house set on top of things which float. I also discovered that it is one of the most incredible places on earth, perhaps even a small taste of heaven. Imagine a place surrounded by tranquil water the color of a border collie's eyes...a place that's glazed with golden sunlight, warm as a donut from a baker's oven...a place where each night, every soul is kissed goodnight by a restful sunset. And if someone can do that, they have imagined the Floater. There's freedom to go boating anytime you wish or to simply kick back on the deck each morning with a latte. Not to mention the fact that when we look out our windows, we see blue skies and cotton clouds reflecting on the river, not green grass in need of constant mowing. Dad, especially, has appreciated that.

16

Boat Ride Adventure

When you are pretty sure that an adventure is going to happen, brush the honey off your nose and spruce yourself up as best you can, so as to look Ready for Anything.

WINNIE-THE-POOH

. . . .

My first season at the Floater was when I was still a pup. That was back when Kari and Zach still had the two boys (Little Buddy wasn't in the picture yet). The boys were the ones who taught me the way of life on the Floater, which I should mention is surrounded by decks and walkways built just above water level. The boys taught me not to get too close to the edge—unless of course I wanted to get wet. They also taught me that while on the decks and walkways, I should never run faster than I could control my legs and paws—again, unless I wanted to get wet.

My second season at the Floater was the year Little Buddy experienced it for his first. And just as I'd done at our land house when Kari and Zach began fostering Little Buddy, the adults allowed me to show Little Buddy around the Floater (of course, there was always an adult with us). But the way I like to remember it is that I was the one who helped acclimate Little Buddy to the Floater. And although we were both only one by human years, being a dog, I was technically older. I felt this allowed me the ability to take Little Buddy under my wing, so to speak.

The first day Zach and Kari brought Little Buddy to the Floater, I met them out at the parking lot. The moment Little Buddy got out of the car, he saw the gigantic tractor. And there was no going anywhere until Little Buddy had the opportunity to play on it, which he did for quite some time. Even though it was roughly one hundred times bigger than he was, Little Buddy was not afraid. He is one of the bravest humans I know. Sometime later, after he tired of the tractor, I led the way to the Floater. I remember how Little Buddy stuck right beside me, the way a good friend should.

He is one of the bravest humans I know.

After showing Little Buddy the inside, I took him around the outside. Since that required walking on the deck, we had a grown-up with us. There were so many enticing things he could see when he looked at the water...schools of minnows, a family of ducks, twigs or sticks floating by, and even his own reflection. I taught Little Buddy not to get too close to the edge, just as the boys had taught me. I knew how important that was, especially since Little Buddy hadn't yet learned to swim. But if he were ever to fall in, I was certain I could rescue him. I remember imagining myself as a champion doggie-paddler, and how I would bravely jump in to rescue him. In my imagination, I was always the one who kept Little Buddy safe.

Also, as the boys taught me, I taught Little Buddy not to run faster on the deck than he could control his little feet. But I remember that as I thought about that further, I decided that since Little Buddy was very young and still a bit unsteady, I made a new rule especially for him—no running on deck at all. And for the most part, given a few reminders, he did very well.

I cannot begin to explain just how good it felt to have Little Buddy at the river house with me. The year before, after the boys had left, I was alone for

roughly five months. Well, not completely alone, since I had Mom and Dad, but alone in the sense of not having a best friend by my side. I needed someone who hadn't forgotten the value in playing chase every day…someone who thought that taking hour-long bubble baths with your bestie was one of the greatest things in the world…someone to take naps with, anywhere and anytime they were wanted. Yes, I needed Little Buddy, and I was certain he needed me.

As I continued showing Little Buddy the outside of the Floater, we came to where Dad kept our boat. When Little Buddy saw it, he became instantly excited. So excited that he jumped up and down, "Boat!" he yelled. "Go ride!" *Yes*, I thought, *what a fun adventure that would be.*

Yes, I thought, what a fun adventure that would be.

As I checked the sky (like any good skipper would), making sure it was clear of any impending storm, I imagined myself taking Little Buddy on that boat ride adventure. I leapt into the boat and then helped my first mate (who, of course, was Little Buddy) into the boat too. Next, I chose two life jackets from beneath the seat—a large for me, a small for him. We helped each other put them on. Next, I opened our secret treasure map and pointed to the marked *X*, which would lead us to the hidden treasure of the Columbia River. While Little Buddy held tight to our map, I positioned myself behind the wheel and turned the key. The engine started with a roar and water spouted from behind. It was all very exciting. And by the look on Little Buddy's face, I could tell he thought so too. We were going to find that treasure. As I grabbed hold of the wheel, ready to shift into gear, Dad's voice brought me back to reality…

"It looks like you two want a boat ride."

Still standing on the deck, Little Buddy jumped up and down. "Go boat!" And I, right beside him, barked as loud as I could. It was the only way I had to tell him that yes, I wanted to go for a boat ride too. Although I knew it would be fun, I remember thinking that it wouldn't be as adventurous as the one I'd have taken Little Buddy on, but at least I had my first mate...and he was my real treasure.

Dad hollered to Mom, Kari, and Zach, and within minutes we were all piled in the boat. After we'd fastened our life jackets, Dad started the engine and water spouted from the motor.

"Let's ride the river," he yelled.

There's always been a lot to love about Dad, but one thing I've appreciated is his sense of adventure. One of his favorite quotes is by Johann Wolfgang Von Goethe, "Plunge boldly into the thick of life, and seize it where you will, it is always interesting."

"Plunge boldly into the thick of life, and seize it where you will, it is always interesting."

Perhaps that's where I get my sense of adventure.

Dad's boat ride was great fun. Little Buddy sat beside me—smiling, hands on the rail, the wind blowing through his hair, completely fearless. And, of course, giggling the whole while.

17

A Smallish Nap

Let's begin by taking a smallish nap or two.

Winnie-the-Pooh

. . . .

After boating for nearly two hours, we returned to the Floater exhausted. Little Buddy and I were so tired that we went indoors, curled up side by side, and took a nap. Mom always says, "Play hard, nap harder." And on that particular day, we did.

How to Take a Perfect Nap

1. A nap should always include your best friend.

2. Naps are best taken in a mutually agreed upon location. (A bed, the floor, a couch. Really, just about anywhere.)

3. Make a vow before you fall asleep that if one wakes before the other, the one who first wakes will remain quiet so as not to wake the other.

4. The bigger (and furrier) friend should sleep facing the back side of the smaller (less furry) friend, allowing his body to cradle them. There will be times however when the big furrier friend will want to trade places and be the one cradled.

5. The bigger friend should wrap his arm (or paw) around the smaller friend, which helps that friend feel secure. Likewise, the smaller friend may hold on to that arm (or leg) and paw to do the same. Places may always be traded.

6. Sometimes it's fun to nap while facing each other. Please note it may take longer to fall sleep, as there's a higher chance that a bout of giggles or silliness will occur.

7. If there are no pillows available, one friend should offer himself to be used as one. Tummies work especially well for this.

8. It is also recommended that the two nappers wear matching pajamas. By doing so, it's very likely they'll share the same dream.

When Little Buddy and I woke, I heard Mom and Kari's laughter coming from the living room. I jumped out of bed, excited to see what was going on. Little Buddy followed close behind. When we reached the living room, it was easy to see that Mom was preparing for one of our photo shoots—her camera was ready, and a stack of clothes was on the coffee table that looked to be my size. The tags were still on, so I could tell they were new. I then noticed another stack of clothes that were also new. And that stack looked to be the perfect size for Little Buddy. I also noted that the two stacks of clothes matched each other. I remember the excitement I felt in anticipation of what was about to transpire.

I remember the excitement I felt in anticipation of what was about to transpire.

Mom chose an outfit from each stack (matching, of course), and waved them in the air. "Who wants their picture taken?" she called. Little Buddy jumped up and down while shouting, "Me picture! Me picture!" And as for me, I was game. I always enjoyed photo shoots with Mom (not to mention

the promise of dried-liver treats). But that day, the very first day Little Buddy and I began dressing alike and smiling for the camera, was one of my all-time favorite photo shoots.

After Mom and Kari helped us put on our matching outfits, they placed us in a variety of poses. I remember thinking how wonderful it was to have Kari with us to help. She was the extra hand Mom needed. I imagined it wasn't too easy photographing a big, goofy dog and an active 16-month-old boy.

Since Little Buddy and I looked so much alike, people might have a difficult time knowing who was who.

Mom must have taken a hundred photos while Little Buddy and I posed reading books, playing catch, making funny faces, and just acting silly...all while dressed as twins. I'll admit, I remember thinking that since Little Buddy and I looked so much alike, people might have a difficult time knowing who was who (keep in mind that I was only sixteen months too).

The pictures turned out so well that Mom posted many of them to my Instagram account. Although I'd always enjoyed sharing pictures of me, it was far more fun sharing pictures of Little Buddy and me together.

18

The Heart of a Sister

*A sacrifice to be real must cost, must
hurt, must empty ourselves.*

MOTHER TERESA

. . . .

One night, after Little Buddy had gone to bed, I stayed up with the adults and was resting on the deck. I remember the sky being magnificent. As the sun slipped below the trees, it left behind a swirl of color. The river house neighbors had come over to join us, as they often did. And because I didn't want to be in the way, I positioned myself off to the side but still within earshot. One of my favorite night things to do at the Floater was to lie on the deck and enjoy the breeze as it lifted off the river. Some folks like to read books or watch a movie before bed, but I prefer lying on the deck and thinking about my day. It's my time of reflection, when I think about all I have to be thankful for. It's so peaceful that sometimes I'd imagine myself spending the entire night out on the deck...just me, the river, and the stars.

While I was relaxing, the conversation between the adults turned to the topic of Little Buddy and foster care. The neighbors were curious about how Kari and Zach became interested in fostering. They were kind people and genuinely interested. Here's how Kari answered.

"Ever since I was a young child, I remember being interested in adoption, so it always seemed to be a part of me. And then years later, shortly after Zach and I married, we heard a speaker, a man by the name of Francis Chan, who discussed the topic of foster care. As we listened, he presented a question that tugged at my heart: 'Why are there hundreds of millions of Christians in the United States and nearly half a million children in foster care, yet we are still in desperate need of good foster homes?' After hearing him speak, and doing my own research about the huge foster care need in our area, I couldn't look away. Neither could Zach."

After hearing him speak, and doing my own research about the huge foster care need in our area, I couldn't look away.

When Kari finished, no one said a word. It was one of those moments when someone's spoken words required extra time for the receiving heart to hear.

I admire Kari and Zach, and I sensed our neighbors felt the same. Kari and Zach could have looked away. If they had, maybe their life would be easier. But they didn't. And for that, I'm grateful.

19

Rainy Day Blues

*When late morning rolls around and
you're feeling a bit out of sorts, don't worry;
you're probably just a little eleven o'clockish.*

WINNIE-THE-POOH

. . . .

One day neither Little Buddy nor I seemed motivated to do much of anything. In fact, as unusual as it was, it seemed we were having difficulty deciding on how to spend our day. It was one of those dark, damp, rainy days that made it an inside day. I remember spending most of the morning watching TV. Mom picked up on this. "What's going on with the two of you? You're usually full of adventure."

Little Buddy shrugged his shoulders. I looked at the floor.

"It looks like we need to do something about this." Mom left for a moment and then returned with a pad of paper and pen. "Just because it's raining doesn't mean you can't have fun." Little Buddy and I watched as she made two columns on the paper. "Let's make two lists," she said and smiled. "One will be a list of rainy day activities for you to choose from, and the other, a list of sunny day activities." I remember being grateful for Mom's problem-solving abilities.

Here are the lists of activities we came up with. Well, truthfully, Mom and Little Buddy did most of the work. I just barked if I liked an idea and hoped they understood. I'm pretty sure they did.

Rainy Day Activities

1. Watch our favorite movies
2. Read a stack of books together
3. Take a long bubble bath
4. Play indoor board games
5. Dress up and have a photo shoot
6. Go to the library and get more books
7. Play with homemade playdough

Sunny Day Activities

1. Sit on the deck and just be with each other
2. Take a sunset cruise on the boat with Mom and Dad
3. Play in the kiddie pool on the deck
4. Ride bikes
5. Play on the swing set
6. Take a walk together
7. Play hide-and-seek
8. Go paddle boarding
9. Go kayaking
10. Go fishing (so Little Buddy can catch fish, just like his dad)

20

Autumn in Oregon

I'm so glad I live in a world where there are Octobers.

L.M. MONTGOMERY

. . . .

Summer at the Floater flew by and the leaves began to change. Mom has always said there is nothing quite like the beauty of autumn in Oregon. She loves the orange oak leaves, the burgundy dogwoods, and the red huckleberries; the turn of the tamarack needles to yellow before they fall; and how each leaf and needle casts a cozy hue of warmth and hand-knit sweaters.

For me, fall has always been about change, warm flannel shirts, piles of colorful leaves, and longed-for winter naps…especially with my bestie.

Because the weather was growing colder (and also because I was now a teenager by dog years), Mom decided it would be a good idea for me to grow my mustache out—"But just a little," she said. She was good with that idea for about two weeks, and then she changed her mind.

"Reagan, your mustache needs a trim. But don't worry," she said. "There's no need to go to the groomers. I can do it." As Mom reached for the scissors, I turned to run but was lured back when she called, "You'll get a doggie bone." I sat before her, my insides trembling. "Hold still," she said. "You'll be fine." As I heard the snip of the scissors, I grew increasingly nervous. Finally, I couldn't take it anymore and pulled my head away. That was a big mistake. When someone says *Hold still*, it is likely for good reason. My not holding still caused a slip of the scissors and an emergency trip to the groomers. A dog like me, who must always be photo ready, should never run the risk of having a lopsided mustache. Not only is it unfashionable, it is extremely humiliating.

Halloween 2015 was exceptionally fun. As I've grown, I've found it interesting how our perspectives on life (as well as on many other things) can change; sometimes quickly, and at other times more steadily. The year before I hadn't enjoyed dressing as a puffy orange pumpkin or answering the door for trick-or-treaters who begged for candy. But Halloween 2015 was different, and I can attribute that to only one thing—Little Buddy. There is something special about sharing Halloween with a friend, and it's even more special when you dress up as two spooky ghosts. Mom originally had ideas of dressing me up as Mickey Mouse, as a baseball player, and even Cookie Monster. But when she realized Little Buddy would be with us, her plans changed.

Halloween 2015 was different, and I can attribute that to only one thing— Little Buddy.

The Thursday before Halloween, Little Buddy came for his usual sleep over. It was after dinner when Mom sat down with Little Buddy and me—she wanted to know our thoughts on what we wanted to dress up as. Really, she wanted Little Buddy's thoughts, but I tried my best to add my two cents whenever I could. Mom had several ideas for Little Buddy. "We could dress Reagan as a horse, and you could be a cowboy," she said. Little Buddy shook his head. "Well, you could both be lions. You could be a little lion, and Reagan could be a big one."

Little Buddy shrugged his shoulders. "Maybe a lion."

That was when Mom got an excited look on her face. "Or you could both dress up as ghosts!"

Little Buddy jumped off the couch and yelled, "Ghost!"

The decision was made. Little Buddy and I spent the next half hour trying to hold still while Mom made our costumes. She made sure to measure accurately and cut carefully so that our eye holes ended up in the right places. Finally, when both sheets were ready (and Mom had figured out how Little Buddy could wear his glasses), we headed off to find Dad.

He simply laughed... very hard.

When we found him, Little Buddy yelled, "BOO!" and I barked as scary a bark as I could. Dad, however, did not jump or scream. He simply laughed...very hard.

21

Holidays and Family

Without family, I would have no reason to celebrate.

REAGANDOODLE

. . . .

That November was special. It was the month when my brother Justin, and his wife, Danielle, adopted Linc. That meant I was an uncle once again. I loved Linc from the moment I met him. We had a lot in common—we both had four legs and a tail, and he was covered with fur the color of a caramel latte just like me. But as for our size, I was 40-plus pounds of romping fun, and Linc was no bigger than my favorite stuffed animal. Being small, however, didn't stop him from playing hard and wrestling with Little Buddy and me. I recall Dad saying he was sure the three of us had more fun than the Three Stooges and the Three Amigos put together. Looking back, I'd have to agree.

Thanksgiving arrived before we knew it, when smells of roasting turkey, mashed potatoes, and candied yams drifted throughout our home. The turkey went in the oven before sunrise, roasting until afternoon, when we ate. You would think that as a dog, my favorite part of Thanksgiving would be the meal, which of course I thoroughly enjoyed. But my very favorite part was when our family sat down at the table, and then, one by one, shared things they were thankful for.

That year, Dad was thankful for his lovely wife (which made Mom blush), for his children and their spouses, for me (he said I continuously made him laugh), for Little Buddy, and for the recent addition of Linc, his new fur-grandson. Little Buddy was thankful for Daddy, Mama, DeeDee, Opa, Justin, Danielle, Linc, and, of course, me, his fur-ever best friend. As the others took their turn, I sat under the table at their feet and thought about all I had to be thankful for. I remember being thankful that Little Buddy had come into our lives (though we still had no idea how long he would be with us), and I was continuously thankful for being adopted into a family who loved me and always took good care of me. I was thankful for my new fur-nephew, Linc, and I remember being extremely thankful that Mom gave me a doggie-safe sampling of that Thanksgiving feast.

Soon after Thanksgiving, Mom turned the page of our calendar to December, my favorite month...Did I mention that Mom made that calendar? And that every month features a photo of Little Buddy and me? Mom makes a calendar every year and donates the profits to support foster care and adoption. Not only has she loved me from the moment she adopted me, but she has also truly inspired me. Watching her use her talent of photography to help others has encouraged me to be the most fun-loving, adorable, and entertaining canine model I am capable of being. Mom has taught me the value in using our gifts to help others.

Mom has taught me the value in using our gifts to help others.

Anyway, back to where I was. It's because of Christmas that December has always been my favorite month.

A Single Star

There it was—the star they had seen in the east! It led them until it came and stopped above the place where the child was. When they saw the star, they were overjoyed beyond measure. Entering the house, they saw the child with Mary His mother, and falling to their knees, they worshiped Him.

MATTHEW 2:9-11 HCSB

. . . .

Little Buddy and I (along with Mom, Dad, Zach, Kari, Justin, and Danielle) spent parts of Christmas Eve and Christmas Day together. Little Buddy and I wore matching outfits, the way we usually do, but that Christmas Eve we looked exceptionally handsome. My very favorite part of the day was going to the Christmas Eve service. I hadn't been before (I had never been to church, for that matter). I had never been invited. This year, however, as my whole family (minus me) put on their coats and gloves to leave, I barked and looked at my leash, which was hanging beside the door. Mom patted my head. "Don't worry, Reagan. We'll be back." I barked again, but this time I swiped at my leash. Dad looked at Mom. "I think he wants to go with us." *Yes, I want to go!* I thought and then barked dramatically, hoping they'd understand. Next, Dad looked at Zach, "Do you think it would be all right?"

Zach thought for a moment. "Well, since Reagan is practically human, I can't see that it would be a problem." Then he pulled his phone from his pocket and speed-dialed the pastor. Because Zach often leads worship at church, he knows the pastor on a personal level. As Zach held the phone to his hear, we listened to his side of their conversation. "That's correct. I understand," he said. "That's exactly what I was thinking. Very good, then. See you in a bit." Zach laughed and reached for my leash. "He's saving us the front pew on the left—especially for you, Reagan-D."

Going to church that Christmas Eve was one of the most incredible experiences I've ever had. On our way there, I remember sitting beside Little Buddy in the backseat, wondering if baby Jesus would be at church too. And if he was, I wondered if he might be asleep in his manger. As I was lost in my wonderings, we arrived. And only a few minutes late. It was a special candlelight service, and the lights were dimmed. The candles flickering on the altar and sill of each window were beautiful, making me feel cozy and warm. Little Buddy and I, in line behind Kari and Zach, walked straight down the center aisle toward the front. As we continued ahead, I was so excited that my tail wagged a mile a minute, possibly even faster. Although I tried to control it, I couldn't...except by sitting down, which we did when we reached our destination, the front pew on the left. Because we arrived a few minutes late, we missed the initial instructions.

I wasn't sure what to do, so I did what Little Buddy was doing. I sat completely still and very quiet. It was definitely not the time to bark, which I almost did when I noticed the wooden manger. And inside that manger was a small bundle, which I was certain was baby Jesus. I could not believe it. Baby Jesus was right there on stage in front of me! The manger looked exactly like the manger Mom had on our mantle, only bigger and life-size. Within seconds, two nativity people walked out from behind the curtain. I recognized them—Mary and Joseph. I remember Mary being plain and simple yet beautiful, like the Mary figurine on our mantel. She looked like I'd imagined she would in real life. Together, she and Joseph walked to the manger and knelt.

You could tell by the way they looked at baby Jesus that he was very special. I felt certain he would be loved and cared for by his parents. At that point, the curtains behind them lifted, and I saw what reminded me of my birthplace...the

farm at Estacada. On the stage were two sheep, a cow, and a donkey. My heart felt as though it might leap from my chest. I was so moved and caught up in the experience that I barked—right out loud! Dad scowled at me and yelled (probably much louder than he should have), "Reagandoodle!"

Thankfully, someone from the back of the church responded, "That is no problem at all! It's good to make a joyful noise!"

It's good to make a joyful noise!

From the corner of my eye, I saw Zach shake his head and overheard as he whispered to Kari, "You gotta love our pastor!"

I sat quietly for the remainder of the Christmas play. I watched the wise men, who had traveled from afar, place their gifts by the manger. These gifts, offered in ornate boxes and vessels, appeared to hold great worth. I also remember being astonished to learn that they had made their way to Bethlehem by following a single star. One star. No treasure map. No AAA planner. No Google Earth. And as I pondered on Mary and Joseph, my mind could not comprehend the privilege they had in raising the King of the world. It was far too amazing. I will never forget how that performance touched my heart and changed me forever.

My second favorite part of that Christmas Eve began when my family returned home from church. Even though Little Buddy and I were tired, we stayed up for a while and sat by the fire. As we drank warm almond milk, Little Buddy shared his excitement of how he couldn't wait until morning. He was convinced there would be presents beneath the tree especially for him. And he was right. There were even some for me. While he continued talking, my mind wandered back to the birth of Jesus, and how his birth was so special that it changed the course of history. I had never heard of a birth that special. As we sat cozily together, we ate as many Christmas cookies as we could, hoping we wouldn't get caught. Thankfully, Little Buddy saved three for Santa.

23

An Incredible Gift

One small gift has the power to change a lifetime.

REAGANDOODLE

. . . .

December 2015 brought even more reasons for it to remain my favorite month. First, that was when my Instagram account grew to such popularity that Mom, Little Buddy, and I began receiving all kinds of media attention (which, I humbly say, hasn't shown signs of stopping). News about us even crossed oceans to places such as Australia, Italy, Ireland, and the UK. But as much fun as it's been, it really hasn't been about being popular or being on TV. It's about drawing attention to a cause that needs our support and to all the children who need love and a place to call home. Otherwise, all the attention in the world would mean nothing. So every time I get dressed up with Little Buddy and Mom takes our picture, I smile not only at the camera, I smile on my inside and think of all the children we can help.

Finally, that December was especially memorable because it was on the fourteenth that Little Buddy gave Mom and Dad a present we will never forget. I can still hear Little Buddy shouting, "Huuwee up, Opa, DeeDee—huuwee up and open pwesent!" What Mom and Dad unwrapped that day was a gift that changed each of our lives. It was a framed poster with the following words, *Daddy Zach and Mama Kari want to adopt me. Will you be my forever DeeDee and Opa?* It was one incredible gift and certainly a surprise. After Mom and Dad caught their breath, Kari announced how the judge had changed Little Buddy's long-term plan to that of adoption. Kari and Zach promised to do everything possible to ensure they would be Little Buddy's forever parents. As the unknowns began to lessen, my heart filled with joy.

All the excitement about Little Buddy's anticipated adoption resulted in something else exciting—once I'd put two and two together, I realized I would once again be an uncle. I would officially be Little Buddy's forever uncle, and he, my forever nephew. And I will never forget how much I liked the word *forever*. It meant that this time, my being an uncle would never have to end.

> *Forever, I've learned, is a very good word.*

Forever, I've learned, is a very good word.

By overhearing Mom and Dad and Kari and Zach, I knew from the beginning that the process of adoption could take a long time. But as you humans say, "Some of the best things in life are worth waiting for." And I am one dog who agrees.

With the first of the year only days away, Mom had our new 2016 Reagandoodle and Little Buddy calendar ready and waiting. As she hung it on our wall, we welcomed January with open arms. It was a time of looking forward, a time of hope, a time of new beginnings filled with things that had never been. Little Buddy and I celebrated New Year's Eve together. We stayed up late, played games, watched movies, ate a lot of food, and then donned our party hats and danced like waves rocking and rolling along the Columbia river—we were movin', dippin', and groovin'. Even though we were running low on fuel when the clock struck midnight, Little Buddy threw handfuls of confetti high into the air. It rained down around us like little pieces of a rainbow. We even watched the ball drop. But once it dropped, so did Little Buddy. He fell asleep on the living room carpet. I snuggled close beside him to keep him warm, and then I fell asleep too.

I couldn't think of a better way to bring in the New Year than being with Little Buddy.

24

Candy Hearts and Birthday Cakes

Any day spent with you is my favorite day.
So today is my new favorite day.

WINNIE-THE-POOH

. . . .

February is often known for pink-lace hearts, holding hands, and plenty of I-love-you kisses. It's also a time for pastel-colored candy hearts stamped with messages of romance and affection. One of my favorite things to do each February is to help Mom (well, more truthfully, to watch her) sort through bags of candy hearts and search for her favorite messages. But since Mom knows how much I like sniffing them, she makes sure to hide them. Each year, however, Mom seems to forget one thing—dogs have 300 million olfactory receptors inside our nose, compared to humans having a mere 6 million. The result? I always know where she hides the candy hearts.

Early that February, I recall finding several bags she'd hidden, and how I'd carefully brought them to her, dropping them at her feet. I barked and wagged my tail, hoping she'd know how excited I was. Somehow, she understood. Looking back, I'm not exactly sure why I liked candy hearts so much, especially since I wasn't allowed to eat any. I believe I've liked them simply for the

joy of watching Mom sort through each bag, choosing the ones she planned to give to those she loved. I remember her sorting each bag until she found every heart that said, *Be Mine* and *Kiss Me* (I had no doubt who she'd give them to).

Even as a young pup, I began imagining that one day I'd make my own candy hearts stamped with my own love messages. So every Valentine's Day, I created as many sayings as I could think of and then added them to my collection. Here are some of my favorites: *I Ruff U, Fur-Ever Friends, I Dig U, Pawsitively Yours, No Bones About It—UR #1,* and *Head over Tails 4 U.* I'd gone so far as to imagine what hearts I would give to everyone. Of course, I'd give Little Buddy the ones that said *Fur-Ever Friends.* Because, really, that's always been my prayer. As much as I've tried not to think about it, there's always that little unknown that creeps up from somewhere deep inside, trying to taunt and remind me how uncertain life is… *"Little Buddy may be here for only a little while,"* it whispers, or, *"Even though there are plans to adopt Little Buddy, anything can change,"* or, *"Don't get attached to Little Buddy. It will hurt too much when he leaves."* I have never liked the unknowns. They are like monsters beneath a bed.

February 2016 was also a time for celebrating birthdays—Little Buddy's and mine. It was the first year we celebrated our birthdays together. It was the year we both turned two.

Mom and Dad threw us an awesome party. The whole family gathered to celebrate. I remember it as if it were yesterday…we had helium balloons, games, party hats, and lots of cake and ice cream. Looking back, I think Zach may have had a too much fun at the party—he untied a balloon and sucked in the helium. After doing that, he didn't sound one bit like the Zach I knew but spoke with a high, squeaky voice. Everyone laughed. Next, I remember Zach turning to me as he squeaked, "Reagan-D, you gotta try it!" I looked at him and barked, and if it could have been interpreted, he'd have heard, *Dude, I don't think so!* I had no idea how my bark would sound post-helium inhalation, and I had no interest in finding out.

When it came time to open gifts, I helped Little Buddy open his by pawing at and ripping the paper, even though he didn't need help or want it. I should have let him open them all by himself, but I was too excited and simply didn't control myself. To try and make up for my poor behavior, I let Little Buddy blow out all the candles on our cake...well, honestly, it was also because I've never been very good at blowing them out—a dog's lips are not designed to purse and blow like a human's. In return (although he certainly didn't need to), Little Buddy let me lick the frosting off his fingers. I've heard it said that give-and-take makes good friends. And if there was one thing I knew—Little Buddy and I made very good friends!

After our guests went home, and I'd vacuumed our birthday cake crumbs off the floor, Little Buddy snuck up beside me and leaned his head against mine. "Whaaagon?"

In return, I nuzzled my head against his. *Yes, Little Buddy?* I wanted to answer.

"Will we always share birfdays?"

I nuzzled him once more and licked the side of his face. *Yes, Little Buddy. That's what besties do.*

I wanted to share all my birthdays with him. Every one of them. I realized that as we grew and changed, our parties would also. A two-year-old's cake and ice cream party would one day become a twelve-year-old's go-cart and amusement park party. From there, to an eighteen-year-old's camping trip with friends only. Later, to a fifty-year-old's golf tournament celebration. And finally, to a seventy-nine-year-old's shuffleboard party. Birthday parties change, as does life.

And that is okay.

Birthday parties change, as does life. And that is okay.

The Usuals

*Gratitude can transform common days
into thanksgivings, turn routine jobs into joy,
and change ordinary opportunities into blessings.*

WILLIAM ARTHUR WARD

. . . .

The pages of our calendar turned swiftly as we journeyed the months of March through August. And from what I'd observed as a canine, it seemed that for humans, the busier their life, the faster their time flew. So if that in fact is true, it would then make sense that if humans lived life at a slower pace, time would not fly by so fast...I believe that is what's meant by deductive reasoning. As much as I've longed to be human, I am thankful for the leisurely life that most canines live. We nap and wake as we please. We play when we have the desire. We have no deadlines. We socialize yet set aside sufficient alone time to keep our lives well balanced.

During the months from March through August, some things remained as usual. One of those usuals were that Little Buddy continued his Thursday night sleepovers with Opa, DeeDee, and me. Thursday night sleepovers, however, actually began before Little Buddy and I were in the picture. They started with the two boys and have continued ever since.

Dad picks up Little Buddy every Thursday evening on his way home from work. And as soon as they walk through our door, Dad, Little Buddy, and I all romp and wrestle until we laugh so hard that we can hardly breathe (I actually wag my tail super fast and require several water breaks). Once we catch our breath, Mom calls us to the table, where I lie beside Little Buddy's chair just in case he "accidently" drops food. (Little Buddy has been carefully taught which foods are safe for me. And, for some reason, these are the only types of food he drops.)

Another one of the usuals were play dates with Linc. Often on a weekend, Justin and Danielle would come to visit. When they did, they brought Linc. And the three of us added together—Linc + Little Buddy + me—always equaled fun. We were family and played like friends.

Aside from the fact I'm basically a canine icon, I actually consider myself quite normal.

Also, looking back at that time frame, even though Mom, Little Buddy, and I had received a great deal of publicity, somehow I managed to retain my humble spirit. Aside from the fact I'm basically a canine icon, I actually consider myself quite normal. I admit, I probably receive more special treatment than your ordinary dog, but I don't believe I fall too far outside the bell curve. Anyway, when *People* magazine featured Little Buddy and me in their April 4, 2016, issue, I admit I held my head (and nose) slightly higher than usual, but only for a few weeks. Once the dust settled, I was back to my humble self again.

During the time frame of March to August, something else exciting took place (although it wasn't particularly exciting for me, since I was left behind). This was when Zach and Kari took Little Buddy, along with both sets of their parents, to Maui for one whole week. And let me tell you, I will never forget how much I missed Little Buddy and how good it felt when he came home. When they returned, Mom had a surprise for

me—a Hawaiian shirt to match Little Buddy's. I remember that right after Little Buddy and I greeted each other with what seemed to be a hundred hugs, I donned my Hawaiian shirt to match my bestie, and we celebrated by drinking pineapple lattes. After Little Buddy had taken his first sip, he looked at me with a pineapple-froth-covered upper lip and shouted, "Ono!"

While I thought to myself, *Ono?* (which to me sounded as if someone was about to be in big trouble), Mom, Dad, Kari, and Zach laughed. Usually I'm quick at picking up on these things, but this went right over my head. Kari must have sensed my confusion. "Poor Reagan," she said. "He doesn't know what to think!" I remember her coming close and giving me a love-rub as a good sister would. Then she said, "It's all right, Reagan. *Ono* is the Hawaiian word for delicious."

I wagged my tail and barked a pineapple-latte-like bark...but in my mind, I was shouting, *Ono!* just like Little Buddy.

26

Don't Forget About Me

*Sometimes, all you need is a hug from the right person
and all your stress will melt away.*

Author Unknown

. . . .

Although March through August seemed to travel along a different time zone for my humans, somehow we all reached September together. And what a September it was. It was a life-changing time.

There is one special day in September I will never forget. Dad was at work, and I was home hanging out with Mom while she checked her email and Instagram accounts. I often enjoyed lying at her feet because she'd use them like hands to massage my back. I could have stayed there forever except that the phone rang. When Mom answered, I immediately knew it was Kari, and I could hear enough to know she was excited, which in turn made Mom excited. "Of course I'll drive!" Mom shouted. "I'll be there immediately! I'll call him right now!" The *him* she was to call was Dad.

After dialing his number, Mom yelled into her phone, "Hurry and meet me at Kari's—we need you to watch Little Buddy! Zach's out of town and can't get home 'til later. A baby girl was born yesterday who needs fostering...Kari and I are picking her up..." Mom was still talking as she grabbed her purse and flew out the door. The next thing I heard were tires squealing as she left the driveway.

Although Mom didn't bother to tell me what was going on, I felt I'd at least gathered the most important information. Kari was going to bring home a baby—a brand-new baby. And that baby, if I'd heard correctly, was a girl.

I spent the rest of that late afternoon and evening home alone. Aside from any noise I'd made, there were only two sounds—the sound of the clock ticking hour after hour, and the dull hum of the refrigerator, which reminded me of how much I would have enjoyed a snack. After waiting late into the night for Mom and Dad, I surrendered and went to bed.

I had no idea how much time had passed when I heard Mom and Dad return home. I jumped up and ran to the door. I barked with excitement, trying to say, *Tell me everything—every little detail!*

Tell me everything— every little detail!

Although Mom didn't share every detail with me, she knelt down and cupped my face in her hands. "You're going to love her, Reagan. Her name is Baby Girl, and she's beautiful—round and pink and soft as a rose petal." After letting me out to go to the bathroom, and giving me a combination late-night dinner and midnight snack, she kissed my head and guided me back to my bed, where I slept like a babe myself until morning.

Mom and Dad had woken early and moved about the kitchen as if they'd already had ten cups of coffee. They were clearly in a hurry. For the first time ever, Mom forgot about my breakfast—until I politely swiped my dish. "I'm sorry, Reagan," she said, dumping kibble into my dish and half missing it. "We need to get to Kari and Zach's before Little Buddy wakes. By the time we got the baby home last night, he was already in bed. He has no idea he has a new baby sister. We want to be there when he meets Baby Girl!"

I refused to eat and sat motionless beside my dish. I'll confess I was sulking. I am not typically one to get his nose pushed in, but I could see the writing on the wall. Baby Girl enters, canine disappears. On account of her I had already

nearly missed my breakfast. I continued sitting by my food dish and watching Mom as she raced about the kitchen. She hadn't mentioned one word about me going with them, and I did not wish to be left home all alone again. I stared at Mom. "What's the matter, Reagan? Why aren't you eating?" I refused to answer, hoping my silent treatment would effectively convey my message. But then Mom reached down and gave a quick rub to my ear. "You'd better hurry and eat. I'm sure you don't want to be late either!"

I never did find out if it was my silent treatment that worked or if I had been included all along.

Dad slid behind the steering wheel while Mom opened the back door long enough for me to jump in. Once she was seated and buckled, we were off. I could hardly wait to meet this baby. While Dad drove, I imagined we were the three wise men traveling to meet baby Jesus, experiencing the thrill, the excitement, and the anticipation just as they must have felt.

27

Baby Girl

Sometimes God brings miracles wrapped in tiny pink bundles.

REAGANDOODLE

. . . .

Because Mom and Dad weren't sure if Little Buddy was awake yet, they didn't knock when we arrived. Instead, Dad slowly turned the door knob and we snuck in. The house was quiet, which answered the question about Little Buddy—he was still asleep. But with the scent of fresh coffee and donuts greeting us at the door, we knew Kari and Zach were up and about.

After closing the door behind us just as quietly as when we entered, we heard hushed giggles coming from the living room, which led us straight to Kari. She was smiling while holding a small pink bundle in her arms. Zach was pressed close beside her, smiling too. They were so enthralled with the little bundle that they didn't notice us. All I can say about that is it's a really good thing Mom, Dad, and I weren't three masked bandits sneaking into their home—otherwise they would have had to forfeit all their coffee and donuts. And if by chance they denied having any, this bandit would've sniffed them out...300 million olfactory sensors put to good use once again.

Finally, when we were practically on top of them, Kari and Zach looked up, not fazed in the least. Kari gently stroked the baby's head. "Isn't she perfect?"

That's when Zach noticed I was there too. "Reagan-D," he said softly, still trying to be quiet. "Come close so you can see her."

Even though I was excited, my insides, feeling jumpy, told me I was nervous too. I'd never seen a human baby before. I inched forward. Kari smiled as she reached toward me and pulled me in. "Look, Reagan," she said, lifting the blanket away as if she were revealing a priceless gift. I leaned in, quickly sniffed Baby Girl, and then looked at Kari. She said, "Go ahead, Reagan. It's okay to sniff her."

Kari understood how important it was for me to do that. By smelling Baby Girl, I learned a lot about her. First, I sniffed her hand and arm—she smelled fresh, new, and hopeful. Next, I worked my way up to her cheek. I accidentally touched it with my nose and discovered it was indescribably soft and just as warm as a sunbeam. Then I sniffed her head, which was as perfectly round as my tennis ball and just as fuzzy. As I sniffed her ear, Baby Girl made a funny sound and wriggled in Kari's arms. I think she may have even smiled at me. By smelling her, I sensed she was happy. I smelled no fear. Baby Girl, I knew, already felt at home.

Zach reached out and rubbed my head. "What do you think, Reagan-D?" he asked. I was so excited and already very much in love with Baby Girl that I barked. It was, however, not a hushed bark as everyone would have preferred. Unfortunately, it was loud enough that I'd scared Baby Girl and made her cry. I also woke Little Buddy. Ashamed and embarrassed, I tucked my tail between my legs and ran behind the couch. Zach turned and peered over the back. "Don't worry, Reagan-D. We're all excited." When I finally made my way back to them, Little Buddy was downstairs, standing in front of Kari and Zach and staring at the little pink bundle named Baby Girl.

I stood beside Little Buddy, who, I could tell, wasn't quite sure what to do. Here was a little boy who went to bed the night before an only child in a family of three and woke as a big brother in a family of four. There had been no warning. No time to prepare him. As brave and strong as Little Buddy was, I

knew there was an adjustment phase before him, and it would not always be easy. But like I've done before, I promised myself I would be there to help him.

Zach scooped up Little Buddy and placed him on his lap so that he faced the pink bundle. "What do you think, big guy? We have a new baby. Her name is Baby Girl."

Little Buddy reached out and touched her gently. "Baby Girl," he said.

"That's right," said Kari. "I love how gentle you are. You're already a wonderful big brother."

Little Buddy smiled and then tucked his finger in Baby Girl's hand. When she squeezed reflexively, Little Buddy's eyes grew big as baseballs. "Mama! Baby Girl hold my hand!"

"Of course she did," Kari answered. "Baby Girl already loves you."

Still holding her tiny hand, Little Buddy looked at Kari, "Is Baby Girl forever?"

Kari leaned over and kissed Little Buddy on his head. "Baby Girl was placed in our lives to love and care for as long as that may be."

. . . .

Over the years, I've learned that no one knows the future. But I've also learned that we can trust the One who created it, the One who holds it. And when we trust, we have no need to fear the unknowns. Our heavenly Father sees far into our future to places we cannot see—he sees those things we cannot begin to imagine.

> God can do anything, you know—far more than you could ever imagine or guess or request in your wildest dreams! He does it not by pushing us around but by working within us, his Spirit deeply and gently within us (Ephesians 3:20).

Epilogue

. . . .

One evening after the manuscript for this book was complete, Mom, Dad, and I received the most incredible news. Upon hearing it, I knew this story wasn't finished—it needed one more thing. An epilogue.

This is what we heard: After nearly three years of pushing through the unknowns, Kari and Zach received the news that Little Buddy's adoption would soon be official. It would finally be complete. The ending of their unknowns meant the beginning of a new journey—a forever journey.

On December 20, 2017, in a small courtroom filled with just our family and a few close friends, Little Buddy's adoption took place. I was right beside him to celebrate. Little Buddy and I wore our finest matching outfits...and I am not too shy to say that we really did look fine. We were handsome in every sense of the word. Even the judge said so. We'd had our hair cut and trimmed the day before so that we looked our best (I even hid Mom's scissors to ensure I went to the groomers—I wasn't about to risk a lopsided mustache for *this* celebration).

My heart filled with joy as I listened to the judge. She explained to Little Buddy that he was especially chosen by Kari and Zach, and then she went on to say how very much Little Buddy was loved and cherished and wanted by them. After Little Buddy said he understood, the judge explained that starting at that very moment, not only would Little Buddy share Zach and Kari's hearts and home, but he would also share their last name. Forever. After clearing her throat, the judge smiled at Little Buddy and announced, "You are now their forever son, and they are your forever parents." Then the judge placed her gavel in Little Buddy's hand, guiding him as he struck the wood block. While everyone cheered, the judge shouted above the noise, "And nothing will change that!"

"You are now their forever son, and they are your forever parents."

I was so caught up in the moment, my heart bursting full of every happy emotion I could possibly feel, that I barked out loud for everyone to hear. That was when Little Buddy wrapped his arms around me and gave me the biggest kiss. And of course, I kissed him back (which coming from me, was more like a lick).

Little Buddy And Reagan's Favorite Things

. . . .

Favorite matching outfit:

Dinosaur pajamas

Favorite movies:

Veggie Tales, Cars, and especially reruns of family home videos

Favorite books:

Jesus Storybook Bible and *Oh, Where Is My Hairbrush? and Other Silly Songs*

Favorite drink:

Almond milk lattes (see recipe)

Favorite games:

Candy Land and Chutes and Ladders

Favorite breakfast foods:

Little Buddy likes Cheerios with bananas and honey;
Reagan likes Mom's homemade Woofles (see recipe)

Favorite foods, snacks, and treats:

Little Buddy likes pizza, fried rice, cottage cheese, smoothies,
black licorice, and carrot sticks with natural peanut butter and hummus;
Reagan likes raw dog food, as well as homemade frozen peanut butter banana
cubes and gourmet peanut butter oatmeal banana dog treats (see recipes)

Favorite sports teams:

Little Buddy loves the Nebraska Huskers football team and
likes wearing his "Herbie mascot shirt";
Reagan roots for the Los Angeles Dodgers just like Mom,
and he even has his own uniform

Favorite activity:

Little Buddy and Reagan both enjoy playing
with homemade playdough (see recipe)

Favorite songs:

Although Little Buddy and Reagan like both of these songs,
Little Buddy especially enjoys "Jesus Loves Me,"
and Reagan, "Jesus Loves the Little Children"

What Do Little Buddy and Reagan Want to Be When They Grow Up?

. . . .

Little Buddy wants to be a policeman. He would like to wear a uniform with a hat and help keep people safe. He also thinks it would be fun to drive a police car really fast so he can catch the bad guys. He says that giving out speeding tickets would probably be fun too.

Reagan wants to be a therapy dog. His mom, however, reports that even if Reagan never becomes a certified therapy dog, he is at least a "virtual therapy" dog by taking people's minds off their troubles when they see him online. Reagan, however, prefers to view himself as Canine Commander-in-Chief of his Smile and Hope Enhancement Services.

Recipes

. . . .

Gourmet Peanut Butter, Oatmeal, Banana Dog Treats

   2 cups quick or old-fashioned oats (not instant)
   2 medium bananas, peeled and quartered
   1 cup creamy peanut butter

Preheat oven to 350°.

Place the oats in a food processor and grind to a fine powder. Add the bananas and peanut butter to the food processor and pulse into dough. Roll out the dough on a nonstick surface to about a ¾-inch thickness.

Use a cookie cutter or inverted glass to cut out the treats, and then place them on a nonstick baking sheet. Bake for approximately 12 minutes or until golden brown.

Note: The treats will stay fresh in sealed container (unrefrigerated) for approximately 4 to 5 days. The treats may also be frozen to extend freshness.

Frozen Peanut Butter Banana Cubes

32 oz. all-natural vanilla yogurt
1 banana, peeled and mashed
2 T. creamy peanut butter
2 T. honey

After blending all of the ingredients in a blender, use a small spoon to fill ice cube trays. Freeze for 3 hours. Once frozen, place cubed treats in an airtight freezer container. Remove individually as your dog desires.

Homemade Oatmeal Playdough

This playdough is not intended to be eaten. However, if it is ingested, it's not harmful to children or dogs.

2 cups quick oats
1 cup flour
1 cup water

Combine all of the ingredients in a large bowl. With your hands, mix and knead until smooth. Store in the refrigerator for several days in a sealed container.

Mom's Homemade Oat Woofles

1½ cups oat flour
   (you can grind dry oats in a blender to make oat flour)
2 tsp. baking powder
½ tsp. salt
Dash of cinnamon
¾ cup milk of choice (cow, nut, coconut)
   at room temperature
5 T. melted butter
   (or 5 T. melted coconut oil)
2 eggs
2 T. maple syrup
1 tsp. vanilla

Mix the dry ingredients in large bowl. In a second bowl, mix the wet ingredients and then pour them into the dry. Stir until combined. Let the batter rest 10 to 12 minutes.

Plug in a waffle iron (depending on the iron, coat with baking oil beforehand). When it's ready, stir the batter once more and then pour some onto the heated iron and the close lid until golden brown.

Remove to eat or place on a cooling rack. Extras can be frozen in airtight container.

Almond Milk Latte

This is a non-caffeinated beverage especially for children and dogs who can drink almond milk. No worries if you don't have a special latte maker or frother. A delicious, frothy latte can be made with a simple lidded glass jar and a microwave.

1 cup all-natural vanilla almond milk
Dash of cinnamon (optional)

Place the almond milk in a lidded glass jar and securely fasten the lid. (A pint canning jar with a lid works well.) Vigorously shake the milk and then remove lid.

Place the jar in the microwave for approximately one minute or until the milk has reached the desired temperature. While using a spoon to hold back the froth, pour the almond milk into a mug and then spoon the froth on top. Sprinkle with a dash of cinnamon if desired.

More About Foster Care

. . . .

To learn more about foster care and adoption,
or what you can do to help, please refer to the following websites:

AdoptUSKids:
adoptuskids.org/adoption-and-foster-care/
overview/adoption-from-foster-care

Bethany Christian Services:
bethany.org/adoption/foster-care-adoption

JasonJohnsonBlog.com

A portion of the proceeds from the sale of this book
will be donated to help support the needs of
foster care and adoption.

Little Buddy, Me, and Baby Girl Make Three

. . . .

My life is full of surprises. First, I met Little Buddy, and then he became a permanent part of our family. But God wasn't done there.

Little Buddy and I are going to get a baby sister. We are so excited but also a little nervous. This is going to change our lives in a BIG way.

I can't wait to tell you all about it next year!

Your friend,

Reagan

Join Reagan and Little Buddy in a new children's book,
Reagandoodle and Little Buddy Welcome Baby
Coming February 2019

About the Authors

· · · · · · · · · · · · ·

Sandi Swiridoff is the "momager" of @Reagandoodle on Instagram. She and her husband, Eric, have two grown children and one famous fur-son (Reagan, of course). They are also very proud grandparents (one of their grandchildren being Little Buddy!). Besides spending time with her family, Sandi's greatest joy is using her gift of photography to bring smiles and encouragement to others while benefiting children in foster care.

· · · · · · · · · · · · ·

Wendy Dunham is an award-winning inspirational children's and middle grade author, a registered therapist for children with special needs, and a blessed mamma of two amazing grown-up kids. She is the author of two middle-grade novels: *My Name Is River* and its sequel, *Hope Girl*. She has a series of early readers titled The Tales of Buttercup Grove. And with *Reagandoodle and Little Buddy: The True Story of a Labradoodle and His Toddler Best Friend*, Wendy writes as the voice of Reagandoodle. Please visit her website at wendydunhamauthor.com.